GREAT KITCHENS

DESIGN IDEAS FROM
AMERICA'S TOP CHEFS

ELLEN WHITAKER, COLLEEN MAHONEY, WENDY A. JORDAN

PHOTOGRAPHS BY GREY CRAWFORD

The Taunton Press

Publisher: JIM CHILDS

Acquisitions Editor: STEVE CULPEPPER

Editorial Assistant: CAROL KASPER

Art Director: PAULA SCHLOSSER

Designer: SUZANNE NOLI

Layout Artist: LYNNE PHILLIPS

Photographer: GREY CRAWFORD

Illustrator: SCOTT BRICHER

The Taunton Press
Inspiration for hands-on living™

Text © 2001 by Ellen Whitaker, Colleen Mahoney, and Wendy A. Jordan
Photographs © 2001 by The Taunton Press, Inc.
Illustrations © 2001 by The Taunton Press, Inc.

Printed in the United States of America
10 9 8 7 6 5 4 3 2 1

Great Kitchens was originally published in harcover in 1999 by The Taunton Press, Inc.

The Taunton Press, Inc., 63 South Main Street, PO Box 5506, Newtown, CT 06470-5506
e-mail: tp@taunton.com

Distributed by Publishers Group West

Library of Congress Cataloging-in-Publication Data
Whitaker, Ellen.
      Great kitchens : at home with America's top chefs / by Ellen Whitaker,
Colleen Mahoney, Wendy A. Jordan ; photographs by Grey Crawford.
            p.   cm.
      ISBN 1-56158-534-3 paperback
      ISBN 1-56158-287-5 hardcover
      1. Kitchens. 2. Cooks—United States. I. Mahoney, Colleen. II. Jordan, Wendy A. III. Title.
TX653.W54   1999
643'.3—dc21   99-32457 CIP

To our grandmothers:

Charlotte Beraux Wünsch, Helen Hawley Reinheimer,

Mary Bell, Pearl Mahoney,

Julie F. Greenebaum, and Alma R. Adler.

We treasure the recipes they wrote down

as well as the memories of great food they prepared

with a pinch of this, a teaspoon of that,

and more than a dash of culinary inspiration and love.

Acknowledgments

First and foremost, we'd like to thank the chefs who are featured in Great Kitchens. They are, indeed, great people, kitchen designers, and raconteurs, as well as great chefs. Special recognition to Hubert Keller, Jean-Pierre Moullé, and Paul Bertolli, for giving of their precious time even before the book had a publisher. We must also mention the chefs' families, who added so much life to the book-writing process as they generously welcomed us into their homes.

The chefs' "other" families—their assistants and staffs—deserve untold thanks, too, for being so accessible, efficient, and friendly. We could not have finished, or perhaps even started, this book without the administrative glue they so unstintingly provided.

We would like to express our appreciation to The Taunton Press for recognizing the value of our idea and for bringing the material to readers so effectively via this beautiful book. Thanks to our agent, Victoria Shoemaker, for her capable assistance throughout its creation.

Thank you to Great Kitchens photographer Grey Crawford, for sharing our enthusiasm about the book's concept and then capturing that spark that makes each chef's kitchen unique. It was fantastic to have a certified "foodie" behind the camera.

Special thanks to Jennifer Sherman, professional cook at Chez Panisse, who willingly cast her expert culinary eye over everything in this book concerning food, cooking, and restaurants—a task she performed with intelligence and dispatch. Also, our gratitude to Alexander Terry and Laurie Friedman as well as the rest of the staff at Mahoney Architects, for their work on the floor plans, recipe and resource gathering, and consistent support. Thanks also to Frank and Christine Currie, who helped us get rolling when this book idea was newly hatched.

Finally, a huge thank you to our families and friends, who read and astutely commented on drafts, listened to complaints, brought us morning coffee at the computer, encouraged us when we needed it, got us to the airport on time, bought us tapes and batteries at midnight, and generally put up with large quantities of neglect—which we hope was benign.

These wonderful people, for Ellen, are: Carl Whitaker, Andi Sherman, Kent Streeb, Greg McCormick, Anna Whitaker, Adie Whitaker, Nancy Hughes, and baby Annika Streeb, who had the good sense to be born three hours after a book photo shoot. Colleen would like to thank: Herold and Connie Mahoney, Corrine Mahoney, Jonathan Tower, and the Davisons—Don, Kerry, Kelly, and Colin, for support while she was away traveling for the book. Wendy's gratitude goes to: Doug Jordan, Heather Jordan, and a host of others who probably will join her at a fine restaurant to toast the publication of this book.

Contents

Introduction

Have you ever wondered what the home kitchens of great chefs look like or how they are organized and laid out? Have you ever thought about which kitchen equipment the chefs consider essential, and what these culinary trendsetters like to cook when they're not at work?

Great Kitchens is the result of an inspiring year spent visiting with some of the nation's greatest chefs in their own homes to answer these and other questions. Each chef in the book has an expert, yet individual, approach to fine cooking. We suspected that each would offer different insights into how to design the perfect kitchen, and that's what we discovered.

The home kitchens of the 26 chefs in this book run the gamut from a high-tech city townhouse kitchen to a colorful room filled with whimsical art pieces and a lipstick-red stove to a mellow space with a cook-in fireplace in an ancient limestone farmhouse. These kitchens are alike only in the richness of knowledge, experience, good sense, and enthusiasm put into their creation.

Some of these kitchens are the result of new home construction; many are full-blown remodels; others show how to update and improve a kitchen with only minor construction or a few pieces of new equipment. All have features that can be incorporated into your own kitchen. We have also included a detailed Sources section to help you identify products that catch your eye.

A few trends emerged from the design diversity and wealth of ideas presented in the chefs' kitchens. Most of them favor a combined kitchen and dining area that works for family life as well as for entertaining. They opt for higher-than-traditional counters, larger and deeper than usual sinks, generous counter space, a kitchen layout that enhances economy of movement and as much built-in flexibility as possible—components, in other words, that make the kitchen comfortable and easy to use. They use

quality cutlery and cookware and have top-of-the-line appliances, investing in equipment that will endure and perform to their high standards.

But just as there were points of agreement, there were choices in which individual personality and lifestyle prevailed. Interestingly, our chefs were about equally split on the issue of cabinets vs. open storage. Members of each camp put forth convincing arguments for the systems they favor. You'll have the opportunity to consider all sides of this important kitchen organization issue and arrive at your own unique solutions.

All 26 kitchens in this book are dazzling spaces designed to meet the needs of people who love to cook. Yet they also are highly personalized, individualistic spaces. These are not restaurant kitchens, designed and staffed to prepare hundreds of meals each week for the general public; they are kitchens meant for homes, family, and friends. These are kitchens where great chefs take off their white coats and relax; where they scramble eggs for breakfast or roast a chicken for the most fortunate of dinner guests.

They are also kitchens where the kids roll out sugar cookies, where friends sip a glass of wine with their cheese, where people cook holiday dinners together, and where families gather at the end of the day.

To give you a true taste of their personal cooking styles, the chefs contributed favorite at-home recipes to Great Kitchens. You'll find this sampling of great recipes in the back of the book.

In Great Kitchens we share with you what we learned about the best kitchens. We hope you will see parallels to your own lives and homes, and that you will gather up many valuable design ideas to use sometime soon in your own kitchen.

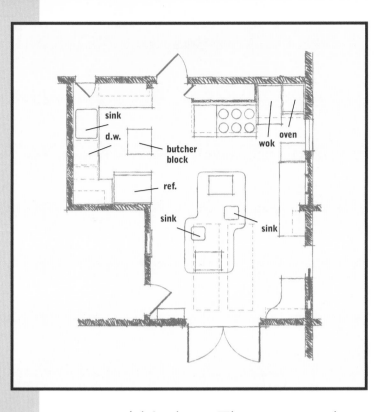

"It's a very textured kitchen. There are a lot of things here. I guess I'm used to it because I've lived here so long. But when people first come in, they say, 'Wow!'"

Ken
Hom

Imperial City

Ken Hom consults for the renowned Chinese restaurant, Imperial City, in London, but he calls both California and France his home—and he travels the globe more than half the year writing cookbooks, teaching, and hosting cooking shows on TV. Ken has authored 15 cookbooks, the most recent being Ken Hom's Hot Wok, based on his popular TV series.

Opposite, This veritable "chef of the world" keeps high-functioning kitchens at home, complete with tools, implements, and ingredients to cook in both Eastern and Western traditions.

Once you see Ken Hom's kitchen, you've met the man. Both make you feel welcome and at ease; both project complexity, harmony, and an extraordinary culinary prowess.

Although crammed with pots, pans, steamers, woks, knives, cleavers, whisks, wooden spoons, spatulas, peelers, chopsticks—and every other cooking implement imaginable—Ken Hom's kitchen manifests a strong underlying organization, a complex order that serves him well.

And though it's no showplace, the kitchen of his blue Victorian home in Berkeley has it all. The range of tools and materials that stock this careful mixture of clutter and calm makes the visitor keenly aware of Hom's own range as an internationally renowned cookbook author, teacher, chef, restaurateur, food consultant, and television personality.

Probably best known in this country as the author of *The Taste of China* and *Ken Hom's East Meets West Cuisine,* Ken is considered one of the world's great authorities on Chinese cooking. He has long split his time between homes in Berkeley and the south of France, but London is the site of his acclaimed Chinese restaurant, Imperial City, where he is the consultant. While his BBC-TV television series *Ken Hom's Hot Wok* is beamed around the world, more restaurant con-

sulting regularly takes Ken to Bangkok, Jakarta, Hong Kong, Sydney, and other exotic locales.

Although he began life humbly in Tucson, Arizona, Ken always ate well. His cookbook-memoir, *Easy Family Recipes from a Chinese-American Childhood,* describes the simple but delicious meals his newly widowed mother prepared practically out of thin air. Ken recalls that even after her long shift in a canning factory, his mother would sauté mussels in curry sauce or steam fish with bok choy and garlic just for the two of them. When the small family moved to Chicago's Chinatown to live near relatives, Ken worked in his uncle's Cantonese restaurant. Later travels in France added new dimensions to his culinary vision. "I've always been intrigued by European cooking. I'm usually recognized for Chinese, but I'm also known for mixing the two, which has become very big now—fusion cooking."

Opposite, Ken's "hot line" features a six-burner, commercial Wolf range, a custom-made wok with its own water source, and an oven specifically designed for making Peking Duck. A super-large copper hood vents the entire line. Ken's large center island, **left,** has easily accessible equipment drawers and two prep sinks to accommodate cooking classes.

Above, Ken likes open storage of his kitchen implements for instant access and because he finds them beautiful. Counters display spoons, chopsticks, and other cooking utensils in decorative jars. Shelves below house larger pots and dishes, while ingredients from around the world sit on upper shelves. *Left,* Ken's kitchen is open to the garden-view eating deck.

The fusion concept plays itself out in his eclectic kitchen as well, where East and West meet: A Wolf range stands side by side with wok and duck oven. Jars of marrons glacés and fermented black beans share shelf space.

The first principle of kitchen design à la Hom is that everything must be in plain view and at hand. "One thing I can't stand about many kitchens is that the cooking tools are hidden away. I think kitchen objects, like pots and pans, are themselves quite beautiful," he says, giving his largest wok a fond pat. "Whenever I travel I research the local cooking equipment and always buy a few things." One of his most unusual finds is a 2-ft.-long Thai coconut grater in the shape of a rabbit.

For easy access to all of those implements, as well as to his vast inventory of spices and bottled or dried ingredients, Ken lined the walls of his kitchen with open shelves, hung a suite of pot racks over-

Left, *Ken's commercial Hobart dishwasher with a 90-second cycle is "the most practical appliance I ever bought."* **Above,** *Ken's ingredients range from French pickles to dried Chinese mushrooms, but the snake is decorative only!*

head, and installed deep undercounter shelves and drawers. Spoons, spatulas, whisks, and tongs are sorted by type and stored in decorative pottery jars on the counters. An extensive collection of Chinese knives and cleavers hang from a specially designed wall-mounted rack. The super-sharp blades are behind Plexiglas, but the handles can be grabbed in an instant.

Ken describes his kitchen design as "an ongoing process," continually refined since he started teaching Chinese cooking at home in the early 1970s. Typical of Victorians, the back of the house was a labyrinth of dark, tiny rooms—laundry room, bathroom, pantry, maid's room, back porch—clustered around a small kitchen. Ken's classes of a dozen or more students simply couldn't fit into the cramped work space. Merging the small rooms to form a large kitchen and adjoining office was an easy call. Popping twin operable skylights into the ceiling netted an abundance of fresh air and sun-

light. A rustic redwood deck and garden are just a step beyond his office. Ken's big, bright kitchen is "very Berkeley—open, casual, warm, and easy-going."

Double French doors separate the office and kitchen but open wide to allow the rooms to function as one space. With the doors open, Ken can test recipes and write cookbooks practically at the same time. "It's a working kitchen," he says simply. It's also the kind of kitchen where people who love to cook feel at home. "Chef friends can come right in and grab what they need because everything is open and exposed."

The extra-large center island with two small food preparation sinks enables classes or parties of friends to cook together (Ken especially enjoys sharing his passion for food with colleagues in an evening of collaborative cooking and out-of-this-world eating). He

Above, Ken prepares greens for steaming. **Above right,** Chinese knives and cleavers are displayed in a Plexiglas rack. With wide French doors opening into the kitchen and to the deck, Ken's study is lined with his cookbook collection, **right.** Here he writes and directs the recipe testing going on in the kitchen proper. Mexican Saltillo tiles unite the spaces, while twin, operable skylights flood the kitchen with sunlight and fresh air.

Left, Ken recently decided to shift his home base from Berkeley to Catus, in Southern France. There he owns a captivating 13th-century stone house, complete with tower, which he has been slowly renovating over the years. In France, Ken decided to let the architectural features of his historic house shine; the refrigerator is hidden behind an old wooden door, ***above.*** Copper pots hang at the ready over his large range with flattop, grill, and two ovens— one small, one large. Oils and vinegars are stored underneath a convenient chopping block table next to the range.

considered installing a chopping block top for the entire island, but used laminate instead because of easy maintenance and economy.

A large cutting board at one end and a pastry marble at the other complete the island's working arrangement. Ken deliberately stationed the pastry marble under a skylight to take advantage of the cool breezes that make dough more workable.

On one side of the room, Ken carved out a convenient but out-of-the-way cleanup alcove. Placement of the extra-deep stainless-steel sink ("people cannot ever have their sinks deep enough") and commercial Hobart dishwasher was dictated by economy: The plumbing for a former laundry room could be reused. The location worked out nicely, since Ken prefers to separate cleanup from food prep.

"Sometimes when I have classes here or I'm testing recipes, the dishwasher is on for six hours, and it's a real advantage to have all those dirty pots and pans out of my working space," he says. (The 90-second-cycle Hobart is one of the most practical appliances he ever bought, he says.) Countertops in the cleanup area are granite to handle the heat generated by the Hobart. Food processors, measuring cups, and bowls are stored in the cleanup area, because

Ken's extensive wine collection, built up over time, is beautifully stored and well organized. Tastings at the rustic table in the stone-lined, vaulted cellar with a fresco of the vineyards are especially convivial.

they're often used over and over while cooking one meal and so need frequent washings.

When the kitchen was first remodeled, Ken used linoleum flooring, "because it was the only thing I could afford," he says. As soon as he could manage to trade up, he installed warm-hued Mexican *Saltillo* tiles. Although Ken admits that the tile can be hard on the feet and legs, he finds it pleasing. He added a swath of commercial-grade rubber matting in front of the range to make life easier on his feet.

Elaborate cabinetry wasn't part of Ken's plan. He made do with simple painted shelves and drawers and cheerful tomato-soup-red laminate counters because he'd "rather spend money on good equipment." As Ken tells it, "From the beginning I bought the best copper pots— very expensive, but the best. I've found that no one even looks at the cabinets because the objects themselves are so beautiful. It's a very textured kitchen. There are a lot of things here. I'm used to it because I've lived here so long. When people first come in, they say, 'Wow!'"

Along one wall is the serious side of the kitchen, or Ken's *hot line:* a commercial Wolf range (six burners, a griddle, and two ovens), a freestanding industrial-size wok, and a special oven for preparing Peking duck. Joey Yick designed and custom-made the super-high-heat wok, duck oven, and gleaming copper hood for Ken, who says, "if you have a big stove, you've got to have a big hood."

If he were buying the Western-style cooking appliances over again, Ken would go for components: a Wolf cooktop, a large, industrial convection oven, and a Salamander rather than a freestanding commercial range. When Ken bought the range 25 years ago, it was a huge investment. It has served him well, but restaurant-style ovens take a long time to heat up and are not energy-efficient. "You only know these things after you have a kitchen and have worked in it. Then you discover what you'd like to have."

But then, Ken Hom is a relentless perfectionist, always rearranging, reevaluating, and adjusting his kitchen, if not his life. Recently, he decided to shift his home base to France and his 13th-century stone house complete with a 14th-century tower, although he also plans regular travel to Berkeley. "Come visit in France," he calls out with a wide smile and a wave. "We'll cook."

Like all French country kitchens, Ken's features a large table right in the middle of the floor. This mellow antique seats 12 people with ease, and is also liberally used as a cooking work surface, since counters are virtually absent. Rough wood beams attest to the house's age, and local pavers create a practical floor in keeping with the kitchen's ambiance. A large dish cabinet displays treasures.

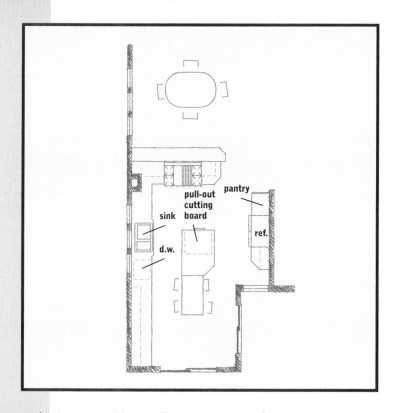

pantry
pull-out
cutting
board
sink
ref.
d.w.

"Although it's still technically a formal dining room, people can look right through into the kitchen. It generates a strong culinary feel."

Ambrosia on Huntington

Anthony Ambrose got his start at New Jersey's Marlborough Inn. In Boston, he worked with Jasper White, was chef at Rarities, and was later at Julien, where he worked under the tutelage of Olivier Roellinger, a three-star Michelin chef. Following a stint at the Bostonian, Tony opened Ambrosia on Huntington, a show-case for his fusion cuisine. In 1995, Boston magazine named Ambrosia the best new restaurant in the city. Tony also has devel-oped a line of tea-based sorbets.

Opposite, *live lobsters delight Tucker.*

Anthony Ambrose

While hurriedly looking for a home to buy just after their son was born, Anthony and Dorene Ambrose happened on the perfect spot. The quaint, 1920s farmhouse was set on several wooded acres bordering a bird sanctuary and promised a reasonable commute to their Boston restaurant. It was also right down the road from the marina where Tony docks his tuna boat—the "Reel Drag"—and offered abundant room for little Tucker to grow and play. In fact, it had everything the young couple wanted. Except a decent kitchen.

Tony's big, white-enamel Jade/Dynasty range sits between the dining room and kitchen. Overhead cabinets without doors or backs display copper pots from Dehilarain in Paris. The cabinetry creates an open division between the two rooms. The Thermador vacuum vent has three speeds and a pair of handy spotlights. Small, square drawers with glass fronts hold dry ingredients. The old brick chimney was uncovered during the kitchen's remodel. Tony and Dorene thought it added to the farmhouse ambiance, so they left it in place as a decorative element.

As soon as the closing documents were signed, they began planning the kitchen remodel. There were plenty of considerations. Tony, chef and co-owner with Dorene of Ambrosia on Huntington in Boston's Back Bay, was accustomed to the best in commercial kitchens, but the Ambroses hadn't budgeted to construct a restaurant kitchen at home. And while Tony's heart was set on a number of special design features that would enhance his piquant, à la minute, fusion cooking style, Dorene was more concerned about where to store the cereal boxes. Furthermore, although Ambrosia's trademark is its stunningly theatrical food and atmosphere, for their private retreat Tony and Dorene wanted simplicity, serenity, and a kitchen appropriate to their old-fashioned house set in a small seacoast village.

To make sure they didn't "over-do" the kitchen, they gave their lengthening wish list periodic "reality checks" by comparing their plans to friends' houses and to residential resale values. On some decisions, though, Tony's excitement for cooking tipped the scale; "choosing a custom-finished, 48-in. stove was pretty extravagant,"

Tony cooks on the range-top rotisserie custom-made by Food Specialists Installations. It's operated either by a motor or hand crank and fits neatly over the range's grill. Behind the range, the counter forms a 6-in.-high barrier to protect guests from the cooktop. The ledge also works well as a plating area. Tony's granite countertops reflect his love of fishing; their iridescent blue and gray flecks remind him of fish scales or the inside of an oyster shell.

*Top, The Ambrose kitchen is designed for Tony's piquant, à la minute cooking style. **Above,** Japanese boxes filled with his favorite spices are always ready in a drawer by the range.*

says Dorene. "What if we had a potential buyer who didn't cook all the time?"

Tony's first step in the kitchen remodel was to open up several small rooms. He moved the refrigerator to an inside wall to create a rectangular, light-filled kitchen with a functional layout. Two sets of sliders open to decks and the surrounding woodland. Opposite, the range and granite-topped serving area form a divider between kitchen and dining room. A custom-built work island and eating table runs down the middle of the kitchen, and the sink sits under a bank of sunny windows.

Tony laid out the kitchen himself, then went looking for a cabinet maker. He was delighted to find J&M Cabinets in Walpole, Massachusetts. Their first task was to fashion the area around Tony's range, which was to be an open link between the dining room and kitchen. Backless shelving overhead and glass-front drawers for colorful spices and dry ingredients frame the range and hood. The wide-open shelves double as a two-sided display area for Tony's collection of lustrous copper pots. He says the arrangement is nice for parties because, "Although it's still technically a formal dining room, people can look right through into the kitchen. It generates a strong culinary feel. You know immediately this is a cook's house."

The two-oven range is a Jade/Dynasty—Jade's residential model. He and Dorene chose the range's white enamel exterior because "we wanted it to look like an 1890s farmhouse range." With their thick, stainless-steel lining, the two ovens reflect heat well and are easy to clean. One oven is convection, the other "still." (The still oven is good for baking delicate soufflés because "you don't want the fan blowing the air around like a convection oven does," says Tony.) A sheet metal craftsman at Food Specialists Installations, Inc., built the stove-top rotisserie. It's operated by electric motor or hand crank.

With two ovens, four burners, a grill, and a flattop, the range needed high-powered ventilation, even more critical because the range is open between two rooms. Tony chose a Thermador—the largest range hood he could get for the space. It has three speeds and two inset spotlights that he thinks are great for seeing the color of the food he's sautéing. For other lighting, the couple installed semi-recessed fixtures with lenses that yield "a nice glow." They also suspended a vintage lamp over the island.

Additional major equipment includes a Sub-Zero refrigerator, a Bosch dishwasher, a Franke stainless-steel sink with two basins, and a Grohe faucet. Tony first selected a large porcelain farm sink, then decided the kitchen sink should have two basins, "especially since we often need one for 'shocking' vegetables" (plunging just-blanched vegetables into ice water to stop them from cooking).

To tie the dining and kitchen spaces together, Tony and Dorene decided on oak flooring and black granite countertops with iridescent blue and gray flecks. Tony's love of fishing is never far below the surface: He admits he fell in love with the granite because it "kind of looks like fish scales or the inside of an oyster shell. It has an ocean effect to it." It's called "Pearl Blue Light." Dorene's design for double-beveled edges worked well in the 1¼-in.-thick granite.

Dorene also designed the white paneled cabinets to evoke the look of a turn-of-the-century farmhouse. One portion of the kitchen's center island is at counter height for use as a work surface; another is a stepped-down table for family meals. The island's massive legs were turned from large pieces of maple; they're built into the island at the work end and are freestanding under the table. The cabinets under the work island don't extend all the way to the floor, so the island looks like a piece of antique furniture.

A hefty, pull-out butcher block slides inside the island. Made of ash, it has a handle custom-made to match the oven's—an arrangement Tony likes. When he's at the range and pulls out his butcher block behind him, he is surrounded by "practically 360 degrees of work surface." To perfect the space, Tony wishes he had put a prep sink in the island.

One feature Tony and Dorene hadn't planned—but like—is the brick chimney they uncovered while knocking out walls. Once exposed, they decided to keep the mellow brick surface as a handy spot for hanging knives on magnetic strips. Most of Tony's knives are by Global. He prefers Chef Inox and All-Clad cookware, which he likes for their durability and even heat distribution.

The finishing touches to the cabinets are custom-cast, stainless-steel drawer pulls in the shape of steelhead salmon. Inside those drawers is a collection of Japanese boxes, filled with the spices Tony

A massive ash butcher block slides neatly into the center island, right behind the range. Dorene designed the island's farmhouse table legs and double-beveled granite.

Left, *Dried pasta, grains, and legumes form a colorful display in glass-front drawers.*

Right, *Open cabinetry between the dining room and kitchen joins the spaces yet makes a pleasing separation. There's plenty of storage space in the dining room for good china and serving pieces. One cabinet holds Japanese dishes for Tony and Dorene's regular sushi dinners.*

loves to use. Describing Tony Ambrose in an article in the *Boston Globe,* Alison Arnett wrote, "First of all, this is a chef with passions, most prominently for Asian seasonings." Tony says his fusion style mixes French provincial cooking with Eastern spices.

Tony recommends that all spices be accessible in little pinch trays, so that the cook can experiment and learn how the spices work together. "If you have to open up individual bottles all the time, you'll never stick with it. You'd never find out that star anise, cumin, celery seed, and nutmeg make an absolutely super combination," he says. Because they're open, Tony checks his spices continuously for oil content, freshness, and richness. He recommends buying a new supply about every four or five months and "reloading" the spice trays. In the future, he predicts home cooks will "increasingly use spices, vinegars, and oils, learning to do more of their dishes in a sauté pan on top of the stove, because it's a fast, flavorful, fun way to cook."

Tony's interest in cooking began in his grandmother's Ohio basement kitchen. "I was always down there with her, making pasta and tomato sauces, passing the time of day." He also spent time fishing with his grandfather. During summer vacations on Long Island, he says, "We'd fish all day, every day. Anything that we would catch, my grandmother could cook, even eels."

After an early start at the Marlborough Inn in Montclair, New Jersey, cooking under Michel Gousfeld, Tony moved to Boston, where he worked with New England culinary icon Jasper White. In 1985, still in his early twenties, Tony took over the kitchen of the Rarities restaurant at Boston's Charles Hotel. "Frankly, I now think I was in over my head," he says. Apparently the restaurant world didn't think so. In 1987, the Hotel Meridien lured Tony away to run Julien, its premier dining room. In that position, he came under the tutelage of Olivier Roellinger, a three-star Michelin chef who had been brought on board by the French-owned hotel group to develop its American chefs. For the next three years, Tony worked alternately in Boston and in Brittany with Roellinger, learning from the best. "I was an extremely lucky young man," he says.

After several years as the Bostonian Hotel's executive chef, Tony felt ready to open his own restaurant. He was all of 31. For two years, he and Dorene worked to get the new venture on its feet. From the million dollar kitchen to the brash decor featuring soaring ceilings, banquettes covered in fish-motif fabrics, and a chartreuse pastry oven, to the menu of such dishes as sashimi, black pearl risotto, and steamed St. Pierre (a white fish) with 14 Asian spices served with quince and yam ravioli, Ambrosia made a big splash on the staid Boston restaurant scene. And its popularity hasn't dimmed. Every year since it opened, it has been listed in the Zagat's top ten Boston restaurants, while *Esquire* magazine called Tony "one of the country's few masters of fusion cooking."

Recently, Tony launched a line of tea-based sorbets—in Lavender Peach, Lime Leaf, and Chocolate Nutmeg flavors. The idea came when he was advised in childbirth class that ice cubes were good for the mother to munch during labor. So Tony took it one step further and froze chamomile tea. Dorene loved the idea, which soon showed up on Ambrosia's menu, and then in stores: A few years later when the Ambrose's daughter, Olivia, was born, Tony was ready with a pint of "Chef Anthony Ambrose Chamomile Tea Sorbet."

Top, Tony loves to take his commercial tuna boat, the "Reel Drag," about 8 or 10 miles offshore to fish for blue or yellowfin tuna. His fresh catch often is featured at Ambrosia. *Right,* The light-filled dining room.

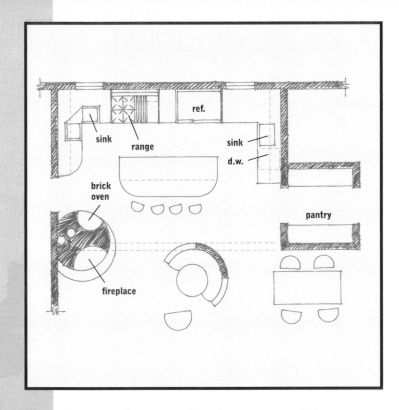

sink
range
ref.
sink
d.w.
brick oven
fireplace
pantry

"For me, a house has to be how you like to live, not how you want to be portrayed to other people."

Restaurant
Nora

Asia Nora

At Restaurant Nora and Asia Nora in Washington, D.C., "organic pioneer" Nora Pouillon presents dishes prepared with the healthiest, freshest ingredients. The International Association of Culinary Professionals named her 1997 Chef of the Year. Nora serves on the boards of Chefs Collaborative 2000 and the Public Voice for Food and Health Policy. She developed a line of dried foods for Walnut Acres, America's oldest organic farm. Cooking with Nora *was published in 1996.*

Opposite, *Nora makes full use of her kitchen island.*

Nora Pouillon

It's not going far enough to say that Washington, D.C., restaurateur Nora Pouillon is an advocate of organic food, environmentally sound agriculture, and living well. *True believer* is more like it. She proves her point through her decidedly upscale version of health food at Restaurant Nora and Asia Nora. Forget the limp bean sprouts and undercooked rice. Nora's warmly elegant restaurants serve exquisite dishes made from fresh, organically grown ingredients. Off the job, it's no surprise that Nora fashioned a lifestyle—and a kitchen—centered around the same ideals.

Right, Nora's versatile Thermador range is her favorite piece of equipment. It has extra-large burners, two oven sizes, a grill, a griddle, and even a wok. The range's stainless-steel back has a 1930s Moderne design appropriate to the house. **Opposite,** The room features unfinished granite countertops, lacewood cabinets, and casement windows. Salt and pepper shakers from the 1940s and '50s sit on the warming shelf.

In 1995, Nora, Steven Damato, and their two daughters bought an Art Deco house with a huge garden in Washington's historic Georgetown section. Its contemporary style made the 1938 house a black sheep when it was built in the tradition-bound area. Though no longer contemporary—the house had servants' quarters and a tiny kitchen—Nora and Steven wanted the property enough to fight for it. Out-bid by just $500, they sweetened their offer by throwing in a dinner for four at Restaurant Nora. They got the house.

The couple's next priority was to update the kitchen. They thought about how they wanted to use the space because, "For me, a house has to be how you like to live, not how you want to be portrayed to other people," Nora says. Her laundry list of "must-haves" ranged from sweepingly general to intensely specific: "First, I wanted a 'good' kitchen, because I'm into food and it's my profession. And we thought a kitchen that opened to a family room would be nice. Then, we wanted to bring in more light with French doors to the terrace." Past the terrace, Steven would have an organic garden.

In the kitchen proper, Nora specified a wood-burning oven, plenty of counter space, high-quality appliances, a pantry, lots of drawers, and three sinks. She insisted on cabinets made with a warm-looking wood, granite countertops, and pure tap water.

First, they opened up the small rooms to create a light, airy kitchen and family space that connects to the terrace. The rounded chimney that holds the wood-burning oven and fireplace also gracefully links the kitchen and sitting areas. A broad, curved partition, which is needed for structural support, echoes the lines of the chimney, hugs the family room seating area, and subtly separates it from the dining room. Refinished, bleached oak floors tie the space together.

Major appliances ring the perimeter of the 8-ft. by 17-ft. kitchen. At the center is a generous island with an unbroken expanse of countertop for food preparation, eating, and more: Nina, 12, and Nadia, 9, "like to help me in the kitchen, and they need space for their papers

and drawings," Nora says. The island also works well as a buffet for parties. The countertop is set at 37 in.—1 in. higher than is customary; the extra height allows "you to chop and not hurt your back," Nora says. The working side of the island houses a Traulsen wine refrigerator and two large, built-in recycling bins.

The counters are topped with unfinished granite because Nora prefers a natural, untreated surface. When the unsealed black stone started spotting, she tried all kinds of oil on it, but nothing worked well. Finally she decided to clean the countertops with water and biodegradable soap. It worked. "The unfinished granite now feels wonderful—very warm and silky to touch."

Right, The open family room bridges the space between kitchen and patio. Metal bar stools are Italian. Seating is built into a wall whose rounded shape echoes that of the chimney. **Below,** A HearthCraft wood-burning pizza oven is set into the kitchen side of the cylindrical chimney. Nora uses her oven to prepare such dishes as roast chicken with root vegetables and peppers.

Nora chose "sunny," warm brown lacewood for the cabinets. With flush doors and rounded counter ends, their sleek simplicity is in keeping with the rest of the house. The lacewood's subtle yet distinctive grain adds character. Nora now wishes she had planned for more large, deep drawers for pots and pans. "I have to stack pans carefully to make them fit," she says.

The versatile Thermador domestic range is Nora's favorite piece of equipment. Sporting four extra-large burners, a grill, a wok unit, a griddle, and two self-cleaning electric ovens—one commercial size, one small—the range allows Nora to cook however she likes. The burners can be turned down very low, and the small oven is perfect for family meals. It also doubles as a plate warmer. Nora loves her big griddle because it's fast and convenient for preparing kids' meals.

The range has extras, too. When the griddle's not in use, a cutting board fits over it. There's also a warming shelf with heat lamp. And many of the stove parts come off easily for cleaning. Nora likes the Thermador because it functions as well as a commercial range but is better insulated than most commercial ranges, so it's suitable for home use.

The "working" side of Nora's island contains lots of drawers, a Traulsen wine refrigerator, a microwave, and recycling bins. On top, there's room for everyone in the family to use a cutting board on the big island. Floors are bleached oak.

The custom-made Thermador hood has a powerful, two-speed fan and exhausts out to the roof. Nora says she should have built the hood a little wider, though, because some smoke still escapes into the room.

Positioned next to the stove, the lacewood-paneled Thermador refrigerator has three compartments with separate thermostats to store different types of food. The refrigerator-door spigot dispenses pure water—in fact, the main pipe to Nora's house has a mechanism that double-filters all incoming water and treats it with infrared light to kill bacteria.

For parties or family dinners on Sunday, Nora uses her HearthCraft wood-burning oven. It's great for baking appetizer pizzas—favorites include garden-fresh tomato and basil, or a crust simply brushed with olive oil and topped with garlic and rosemary. She uses the oven frequently in winter to roast chicken or duck with root vegetables.

Nora wanted three stainless-steel sinks for large-scale cooking—an extra large, deep one for cleanup and a double sink, good for simultaneously cleaning quantities of vegetables and lettuce. Metal-lined tilt-out drawers under the sink aprons keep damp sponges and vegetable scrubbers handy but out of the way.

The stainless-steel cleanup sink in a corner of the kitchen features a built-in drainboard for drying large pots and bowls. Nora's Finnish ASKO dishwasher uses very little water—another nod to the environment. Next to the cleanup area is a small pantry for storing cases of food, large platters, vases, and small appliances.

As for small appliances, Nora favors her De Longhi food processor, because it has a superior vegetable and juicer attachment. She uses only stainless-steel (All-Clad), ceramic, and cast-iron cookware. She especially favors cast iron because it supplies iron to the diet. Favorite hand tools are a Benriner mandolin and Global knives.

Nora's strong interest in healthy living was formed during her childhood in Vienna, Austria. At her French school she "learned a lot about eating habits and about food." There, three-course midday meals introduced Nora to the pleasure of simple, well-prepared food accompanied by congenial conversation. It didn't hurt that her parents believed in nourishing foods and plenty of exercise.

Nora's approach to food was polished by her marriage to a Frenchman who, "like all French men, was a gourmand." Luckily, she says, a friend introduced her to Elizabeth David's *French Provincial Cooking*.

When the Pouillons moved to Washington in the mid-60s, it took more than cookbooks and keen interest to prepare the meals they wanted. They needed fresh, high-quality ingredients, too. In U.S. grocery stores "food was plentiful," says Nora, "but nothing had flavor.

Left, *The food preparation double sink is a corner unit from Elkay. A Grohe high-arch faucet has a push-button spray and pulls out to make a hand-held unit. Nora likes the faucet design because it "doesn't clutter the area, and you can get a large pot under it."* **Below,** *Although Steven is the gardener in the family, Nora likes to harvest fresh golden pear tomatoes—and many other vegetables and herbs for use at home or in her restaurants.*

There was no fresh garlic. Bread was bad. Iceberg lettuce was it." While searching for a source of better-tasting meat, she found a Pennsylvania farmer who sold natural beef. "I asked, 'What do you mean by natural beef?'" Nora recalls. Finding out that cattle were routinely fed growth hormones and antibiotics "really triggered my interest and I started investigating what agriculture was doing in this country. Basically, food was not raised for its nutritional content or for its flavor; it was raised for high volume and for how it would look. 'This must change,' I thought. Food is what keeps us alive."

Nora doggedly uncovered sources of healthy, flavorful foods. She also became an accomplished cook. After friends encouraged her to open a home-based cooking school and catering business, her culinary reputation grew. In 1978, she was approached to open the restaurant at a local inn and because her marriage was ending, Nora decided it was time to "go professional." She took the job. At the Tabard Inn, she met Steven, her future partner, and one year later they opened Restaurant Nora in a 19th-century carriage house they had struggled to buy.

Left, Nora's family room, kitchen, and dining room form one large living space. The dining table folds up and the chairs stack to convert the dining area into exercise space. *Above,* Nora collects 1940s Fire-King ovenware and Jadite dishes.

Restaurant Nora's focus was always clear: "From the start, I wanted to do only organic food," says Nora. Twenty years later, it is firmly established as one of the city's favorite special-occasion restaurants, serving such raved-about dishes as fennel grilled lamb chops, Tuscan tomato-bread salad, and polenta-crusted Rhode Island scallops with wild mushroom risotto. A second restaurant, Asia Nora, reflects the chef's interpretation of Asian cuisine.

Nora has not stopped spreading the word about fresh, healthy foods. She has involved herself with food policy at the highest levels of government. She has also worked through the Adopt-a-School program to introduce kids to baking nourishing breads from different cultures. "It's easy to get them interested, because children love bread," Nora states. And she has continued to educate herself. "When I travel, I always visit food markets and farmers to find out how people feed themselves in other countries."

In the future, Nora sees more "global" foods, mixing elements from many traditions and locales. She also thinks the trend toward prepared foods will continue—but using nutritious, quality, organic ingredients. "So, food will go in both directions, both more organic and more 'engineered,'" she says. "There's nothing wrong with convenience foods, as long as they're healthy."

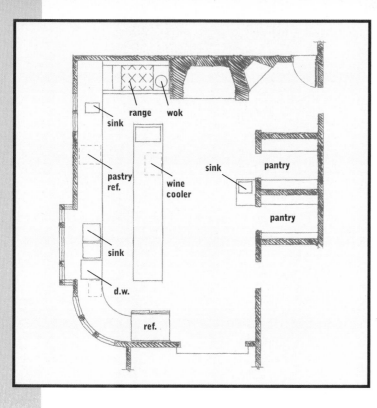

Mark Miller owns five restaurants. After graduate school, he cooked at Chez Panisse then started two restaurants in California. He launched Coyote Café in Santa Fe in 1986; Red Sage in Washington, D.C., and another Coyote in Las Vegas followed. Mark's pan-Asian restaurants include D.C.'s Raku and San Francisco's Loongbar. Mark was named Best Chef in the Southwest by the Beard Foundation, has written nine cookbooks, and developed a line of Southwest food products, Coyote Cucina.

Opposite, *Mark prepares spices to marinate lamb.*

"I designed the kitchen so that when I'm not cooking or writing or teaching, it's very beautiful…. A kitchen can look like a 'garage' if you're not careful."

Mark Miller

"I wanted my home to feel like an old Islamic-Moorish house uncovered in the south of Spain and then completely remodeled with a modern sensibility," says Mark Miller, famed chef of Santa Fe's Coyote Café. "I like a kitchen to have some breadth and history." Overall his house is much more than an ancient desert retreat interpreted with a stunning modern aesthetic. It's pure Mark Miller.

Above, The frescoed walls and ceiling are a soft carmalito *shade; blue tiles face the range's backsplash; the floor is Italian "ceramic stone."* **Left,** *Mark designed the Moorish-style dome inset with colored glass.* **Opposite,** *Copper pots, yellow travertine countertops, and blue window frames make a rich display.*

Mark bought his property—rolling, piñyon-dotted, high desert land—in 1979. Within a month he'd designed the floor plan for his new home and staked it out on the wilderness hilltop. He liked to stand in the "kitchen" looking out its "windows," to make sure each view would be perfect. But with Mark's busy schedule, construction didn't begin until 1994.

About 10 miles outside Santa Fe, the expansive, U-shaped house has a "public area" consisting of the great room and adjoining kitchen, guest accommodations, and a video viewing room. The "private" side has a master bedroom, bath, sauna, and 12,000-volume

library (including 4,500 cookbooks). "Everyone has plenty of space in New Mexico," Mark says. "It would look ridiculous to have a cozy little kitchen here because the minute you glance out the window to the landscape, your whole sense of proportion is completely redefined.

"I designed the kitchen's aesthetics based on its orientation to the living room. These two main rooms in the house are connected by space, but are differentiated by color, ceiling height (it's three steps up to the kitchen), and materials." Both rooms look west to a limitless horizon.

The kitchen proper is about 600 sq. ft. Counting the pantry, wine cellar, and back hall, it's more. Mark has uses for all that space; training chefs, consulting, and writing cookbooks are just some of them. "As a teacher, which is my primary role now, the attention that I can give to a chef in my home kitchen over two or three days is probably equivalent to three or four months of training 'on the job' in a busy restaurant." And, while testing recipes for cookbooks—he has written nine of them—Mark needs lots of room to spread out.

Even when cooking on a small scale, the extra space is valuable. "I tend to work on more than one thing at a time. In most home kitchens, when you're having a dinner party you run out of space. First you bake the cake, getting all the counters filled up with cake stuff. Next it's time to prep the vegetables and marinate the meat, but then the cake comes out of the oven and there's no surface left to frost it on." Mark realizes his 25 lineal ft. of counter space is a luxury, but, "I really appreciate the pure non-

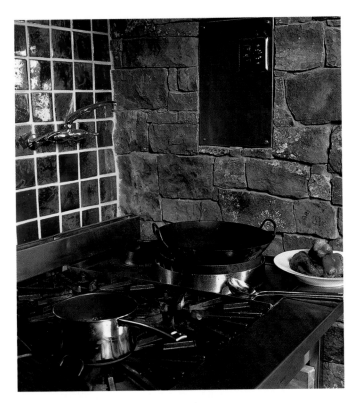

round out the cooking options. The plug-in burners can be used anywhere—for entertaining or while teaching chefs. "Kitchens should be flexible spaces," Mark states.

All the gas-fired appliances use propane, which burns hotter than regular gas. "It's better," says Mark with a grin. "If I had everything going at once, it'd be about half a million BTUs." The range has only one convection oven, but that's all he needs.

The kitchen is divided into work zones. Mark paid special attention to landing spots, to hot and cold zones, and to wet and dry areas. Left of the range is an accessory sink for the cook. Ten feet down the counter from the hot zone, Mark placed his pastry station. To chill the countertop for ease in working dough, he cut off the top of an under-counter Traulsen pastry refrigerator and slid the unit under the travertine counter. It keeps the pastry ingredients—and the work surface—at a perfect temperature. Mark also has an Ice-o-Matic ice maker, a "good idea, if you're going to do a lot of pastry."

interruptedness of it. If I put something down, it can stay right there until it's finished."

The layout of the kitchen is just as important as its spaciousness. At one end of the 30-ft. by 20-ft. room are the range, wok, open fire-place, and pizza oven. The refrigerator and 8-ft.-wide doorway to the great room are at the other. Surfaces for food preparation stretch between the two. Twin dish- and food-storage pantries sit to one side ("I hate cabinets," Mark says). As in a commercial kitchen, the food moves in an efficient line from storage to prep areas to the place where it's cooked.

The arching, 6-ft.-wide Provençal fireplace is made of rustic sand-stone blocks. Spanish-style, inset grills were custom-made. Mark can adjust the height of the various grills to cook a number of foods at the same time, but at different temperatures. The motorized rotis-serie has variable speeds and can hold up to 75 pounds. To the right of the fireplace, a Renato pizza oven is set into the sandstone. On the left, Mark's Montague range has six star burners and an 18-in. grid-dle. A faucet behind the range makes filling large pots easy. A pro-fessional wok, Gaggenau fryer, and portable electromagnetic burners

Opposite, Mark "hates cabi-nets," so he built two walk-in pantries for dry ingredients and dishes. The pantries are arranged by country and cui-sine, since Mark draws on many cultures for culinary inspiration. The ingredients pantry has a root cellar in the floor. A third sink sits between the pantry arches, which are decorated with Renaissance designs. "I've always liked geometric opticals," Mark says. *Above,* The "hot line" has a convenient water source. *Right,* Beautiful pots.

The 36-in.-high countertops along the west wall are made of an unusual, golden yellow New Mexican travertine. Its warm color, sinuous striations, and bits of darker gold, creamy white, and reddish brown create a design that flows around the room. In a bay in the counter, where the desert view is particularly serene, Mark placed his cleanup area. The custom-made, stainless-steel double sinks are 18 in. deep and have a built-in, slanted drain board. A KitchenAid dishwasher resides next to the sinks. Mark says one sink should have been shallower. "It's very difficult to wash dishes way down there," he says.

In addition, there was no room underneath the deep sinks for a garbage disposal. As a final disappointment, Mark's metal-lined herb window garden behind the sinks—meant to soften the five months of winter at Santa Fe's 8,000-ft. altitude—is virtually inaccessible from the kitchen. "The sink and garden thing bother me a little bit," he says ruefully.

It's 39 in. from the counter to the 17-ft. maple butcher block island. The space between the range and the island is slightly less, "so I can turn around and put hot things down quickly," Mark explains. He inset a slab of the travertine at the range/grill end of the island specifically for that purpose. "People build grills without a staging area," Mark says. "Where are you going to put the partially cooked meat when you want to brush marinade on it?"

Mark's island is 38 in. tall. "I know that sounds high, but it's a comfortable working height for most professionals," he says. On the outside of the island, Mark placed his 60-bottle wine refrigerator plus storage space for glassware. This orients guests toward the non-

---

Above, Drawers with cut-down fronts make for handy, visible storage of pots, pans, and bowls. The floor has radiant heat, comfortable during Santa Fe's long winters. *Left,* Storage for sheet pans and small cutting boards. *Opposite,* Mark's butcher block–topped island includes olivewood cabinets for glassware on its "outside." The chef loves his four-door commercial Traulsen refrigerator for its flexibility; shelves can be quickly removed for storing large food items. It's quiet, too, because the compressor is remote.

working side of the island, where they linger, have a glass of wine, and watch while he cooks. The open shelves and drawers are made of lovely, hard-to-get olivewood.

The four-door, commercial Traulsen refrigerator is all practicality. The appliance conforms to the chef's belief that equipment and storage areas in kitchens, even home kitchens, should be "modular," that is, either 24 in. or 12 in. wide, thus accommodating a full or half-sheet pan. "You roll out some dough on a sheet pan, stick it in the freezer for awhile, put it in the oven, refrigerate the baked goods, all on the same pan." He also likes to organize the slide-out pans in the Traulsen by type of product—meat, poultry, shellfish, dairy, and

so on. "Then I know immediately where to look for things. It's like a file cabinet."

The two walk-in pantries are equally well arranged. "One is for dry ingredients, organized on the shelves by country or cuisine, and one for tableware, sorted into sections for ethnic and Continental dishes," Mark explains. A root cellar is built into the floor of the food pantry.

While it may seem that Mark's kitchen has every imaginable bell and whistle, he can instantly zero in on what's essential—"surface areas, knives, and bowls," he says. More than 75 bowls are stored under the island. Knives rest in an angle block on the counter. On the less basic side, Mark's current favorite kitchen gadget is a Japanese

Right, *The arching, 6-ft.-wide Provençal fireplace, made of rustic sandstone blocks, is the kitchen's centerpiece. Wood is stored below. Spanish-style inset grills were custom-made, and the grill heights can be adjusted to cook a number of foods at the same time, but at different temperatures. The variable-speed, motorized rotisserie can hold up to 75 lbs. The kitchen also boasts a Renato pizza oven and a Gaggenau fryer.*

Opposite top and bottom, *Mark loves to use his built-in, professional wok to stir-fry vegetables.*

"fuzzy logic" rice cooker that "knows" how to prepare all types of rice perfectly.

But the kitchen is not just well planned, it's a seductively attractive space, too. The walls are frescoed a soft, deep *carmalito* shade. Shimmering Spanish tiles face the range's backsplash, intriguing Renaissance designs frame the arched doorways, and a luminous Moorish dome with colored glass is set into the 13-ft. ceiling over the fireplace. "I wanted the warmth of the colors in the wintertime here." Though Mark loves the counter space in his kitchen, his favorite thing about the room is its palette of rich, glowing colors.

"I designed the kitchen so that when I'm not cooking or writing or teaching, it's very beautiful. It's peaceful. I don't want to be constantly reminded that it's a working environment. A kitchen can look like a 'garage,' an industrial workplace, if you're not careful."

Mark lent a guiding hand in decorating his restaurants, too. From the Coyote Cafés in Santa Fe and Las Vegas to Red Sage in Washington, D.C., to Loongbar in San Francisco, he put his unique imprint on the space as well as on the food. Born and raised in Boston, Mark made his way to California, where he studied cultural anthropology and Chinese art at the University of California at

Berkeley. After graduate school and a few months at Williams-Sonoma, he seized the opportunity to work for Alice Waters at Chez Panisse. In 1979, Mark opened his own Berkeley restaurant, Fourth Street Grill, adding spices and ingredients from around the world to the "New American Cuisine" he had mastered. Shortly thereafter, his second Berkeley restaurant, Santa Fe Bar and Grill, opened to rave reviews.

In 1984, he sold the Santa Fe Bar and Grill and Fourth Street, and moved to the real Santa Fe to concentrate on southwestern cuisine. There Mark launched Coyote Café, serving food drawn from the region's cultures: Mexican, Hispanic, Native American, and *Anglo.* At Coyote Café, Mark "helped put modern southwestern fare on the food map," according to the *Christian Science Monitor.* He earned a spot on *Life* magazine's list of "most influential chefs of the 1980s." By 1992, he was ready to take his spicy, savory cuisine to Washington, D.C., with Red Sage, which that year was named *Esquire's* "Restaurant of the Year." At Red Sage, Mark introduced Washingtonians to the delights of such dishes as wild morel quesadillas, cold avocado soup, and spiced turkey and venison empañadas. The Las Vegas edition of Coyote Café opened at MGM Grand in 1993.

Then it was time to explore the cuisines of the Asian cultures Mark had studied in school. Raku: An Asian Diner opened in two D.C. locations in 1997, offering casual, vibrant "street foods" from a number of Asian countries. The next year saw the long-awaited inauguration of San Francisco's Loongbar—another pan-Asian concept offering such delicacies as lobster and quail egg soup from Malaysia, sizzling rice crepes with grilled calamari and Vietnamese herbs, and Szechuan beef short ribs. Mark traveled extensively in Asia to collect the art and antiques that create the restaurant's ambiance, combining traditional Asian motifs with a contemporary sense of space and comfort.

Where will Mark's worldwide interests and culinary skills take him next? Wherever it is, he will always have his inimitable desert retreat in Santa Fe to come home to.

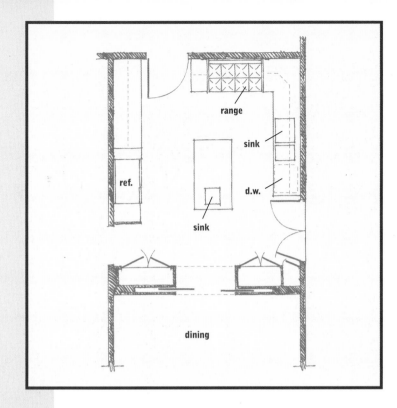

range

sink

ref.

d.w.

sink

dining

"My fantasy was to have no kitchen. That would be the ultimate luxury, since I live in a restaurant kitchen. But the bank said, 'All houses have kitchens.'"

Inn at Little Washington

Patrick O'Connell's Inn at Little Washington in Washington, Virginia, is a Mobil five-star inn and a widely acclaimed restaurant. There, the self-taught chef offers his "cuisine of the territory, with a twist": superlative, local ingredients served in new, sometimes surprising, ways. In 1992 and 1993 Patrick was honored by the James Beard Foundation, first as Best Chef in the Mid-Atlantic Region, then as proprietor of the Restaurant of the Year.

Opposite, Watch this spot for homemade dog biscuits.

Patrick O'Connell

The Inn at Little Washington, A Consuming Passion, is the title of Patrick O'Connell's cookbook. It's also a neat play on words and a precise summary of Patrick's life for the past 20 years. How else could the self-taught chef have created his over-the-top luxurious country inn and celebrated restaurant from a run-down car repair shop in the rural Shenandoah Valley?

Above, Patrick's compact kitchen blends order, polish, state-of-the-art equipment, and old-fashioned appeal. The backsplash tiles are Portuguese, hand-painted with charming Asian figures. Countertops are elegant but serviceable black granite.

Left, The large lion-head door pulls actually are door knockers; Patrick calls them "vivacious and fun, a nice way to dress up something as boring as kitchen cabinets."

In 1978, Patrick and his partner, Reinhardt Lynch, looked for an affordable property in the tiny hamlet of Washington, Virginia—about 65 miles from "big" Washington. Their goal was to open a restaurant and, eventually, an inn. While leasing a ramshackle garage surrounded by a junk yard, the pair insisted on an option to buy after the first year; they somehow sensed their gamble had promise.

Five years later, the venture was a runaway success, but the commute between their outlying farm and the inn had begun to take its toll. With 24-hour room service and late nights in the kitchen, Patrick and Reinhardt knew it was time to move closer to town. A midnight auto accident with a deer clinched the decision. Again, luck was on their side. They snapped up a small, 100-year-old house for sale directly behind the inn.

In his vivid style, Patrick recalls an original dislike for the house's jumbled architecture, "ruined with a huge, red, horrible, modern chimney on its front." Architect Alan Greenberg, who was designing an addition to the inn at the time, counseled Patrick and Reinhardt to

remove the chimney. They did, but then "there was hardly anything left." In a way, it was like starting over with a refreshingly clean slate, but they didn't want to create anything unexpected or out of character in the small town.

Patrick says, "The idea, when it was finished, was that the house would look like it had always been there. And my original fantasy was to have no kitchen," says Patrick, with wry amusement. "I thought that would be the ultimate luxury, since I live in a restaurant kitchen all day. Then the bank intervened and said sternly, 'All houses have kitchens.'"

If there was to be a kitchen, Patrick wanted an efficient, well-equipped, and pleasant space that would lend itself to formal enter-taining as well as to Sunday lunch with family and friends. While the allotted kitchen space was small, Patrick knew it could be ideal—a simple, well-ordered work area that also expressed his style and sense of fun.

An atrium-style dining room adjoining the kitchen was popped into the house's footprint. Built-in china cupboards on both sides of the doors store a collection of plates and platters.

Adding the dining atrium was just part of the old building's resus-citation. "The grounds and whole house needed a boost, some life and warmth."

Happily, he was consulting at the time with an English decorator and stage set designer who was refurbishing the inn's dining room. Known as a genius with color, Joyce Evans leapt at the challenge of sparking up the drab house. Working long distance from London, she sent vibrant watercolor renderings of her dramatic designs for the house, along with paint chips and fabric samples. "Somehow, in a

Top, *A little bit of history uncovered during the remodel.*
Left, *Between the refrigerator and a stretch of countertop, Patrick placed a trim, floor-to-ceiling vertical storage unit that makes a space-saving repository for spices and packaged ingredients. Knives are handy on a magnetic strip, and the island is just a step away.*

flash of inspiration, Joyce would look at the blueprints and was able to put herself in the space," Patrick says.

Joyce helped Patrick and Reinhardt choose updated colonial colors and integrate them into their plan. The kitchen cabinets' deep royal blue paint was "dragged" for an antique patina. The large lion head pulls are actually door knockers; Patrick calls them "vivacious and fun, a nice way to dress up something as boring as kitchen cabinets." A rich terra-cotta red ceiling and white tile floor give the room a feeling of height—an important consideration for the extra-tall chef. He wanted a tile floor because it's easier to clean than wood, and he rejects the notion that tile is harder on the feet than other flooring materials. "Everything's hard on your feet," Patrick attests. "If you've been standing all day, even sand is hard on your feet."

Tile was also used for the backsplashes, this time Portuguese imports, hand-painted with charming Asian figures. The focus was on a polished, antique, "always-been-there" look. Countertops are ele-

gant but serviceable black granite, which Patrick appreciates for its durability.

Patrick commissioned local furnituremaker Peter Kramer to build the magnificent, maple butcher block–topped table for his center island. Although a true table with freestanding legs, the island was plumbed to hold the kitchen's second sink; the water supply pipe threads up inside one fat table leg and the drain down another. The small but deep sink, framed by the extra-wide maple top, is a handy backup sink and works well for cleaning vegetables. Patrick likes a kitchen island because it's a convenient multi-sided work surface and it's congenial for stove-side meals.

Around the perimeter of the compact, 15-ft. by 16-ft. space, Patrick positioned his appliances. A big, eight-burner Viking range is commercial quality but made for homes. Its two ovens convert to convection. Each oven has a "nice little glass door"—a valuable feature when you own two frisky Dalmatians who prefer homemade dog bis-

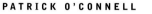

Opposite, *Sliding pocket doors between the dining atrium and kitchen open for casual gatherings. Closed, they create an elegant dining retreat and separate "service" kitchen.* **Above,** *Patrick's "Rose Cottage" is named for one of his Dalmatians.* **Right,** *Outside the kitchen, porch and garden beckon.*

cuits. "Rose can watch them baking through one door, and DeSoto through the other," Patrick says with a grin.

A double, stainless-steel Elkay sink ("it's practical, easy to clean") has a high-arch Kohler faucet, good for filling large pots. Next to the sink, Patrick installed a boiling-water faucet. "Everything should be instant," he states. The quiet KitchenAid dishwasher and Amana side-by-side refrigerator and freezer coordinate well with the other appliances.

Resourceful cabinet design includes an angled corner unit with a lazy Susan below and a deep pull-out compartment that houses a garbage can; when it's closed, it looks like the other cabinets.

"This is a nice one-person kitchen," Patrick says. "You can move around in the work space next to the refrigerator. Here's a landing spot for equipment you're taking out of the cabinets. Dry ingredients are right here. The under-counter strip lights are a good idea, and there's some task lighting, too."

Kitchen features Patrick doesn't like all relate to height and head room. The tall, lanky chef thinks the range's hood is badly placed and has dangerous, head-banging corners. The grid-like pot racks don't work well for him, either. The pot racks and hood are being reconfigured to a "higher" standard.

Favorite small appliances include a Waring blender and a KitchenAid mixer. He prefers French copper pots and All-Clad cookware.

Patrick calls his much-praised, self-taught cooking style "a sort of 'cuisine of the territory,' with a twist. I go for interesting juxtapositions of flavors and textures. And always beautiful presentations," he says. The dining public approves; with just 65 seats, the Inn at Little Washington has received up to 3,000 reservation requests for a single Saturday night. The lucky diners who get in might sample crispy seared foie gras on a wedge of polenta and local ham, surrounded by black currant sauce, miniature timbales of crabmeat with spinach mousse, blackberry vinegar-marinated quail on Johnnycakes, or grilled rack of lamb in a pecan crust.

At home, Patrick takes another route. "What I like to cook at home is spaghetti, deviled eggs, potato salad, roast chicken—'mama' food, unfancy food—the kind of food we don't serve in the restaurant," Patrick says.

Patrick got into cooking while a drama student at Catholic University in Washington, D.C. Like many aspiring actors, he gravitated to part-time restaurant work. After college, Patrick spent a year traveling in Europe, sorting out what he wanted to do with his life. Before going, a friend advised him to buy some local property, so he'd be inclined to return. "In 1970," Patrick remembers, "I plunked down $1,500 for three acres and a mountain shack with an old school bus attached to the rear." It was something to come home to.

On his return, Patrick discovered he had developed a fresh perspective on cooking and on the restaurant business. "Before then I thought people cooked because they couldn't get another kind of job," he says. "Certainly, it was without any prestige and didn't require creativity. All you needed were deep fryers and maraschino cherries." But in France, particularly, Patrick began to understand cooking as an art form, something that utilized all your creative talents—and a career that could be very exciting.

Once back in Virginia, his first move was to sell the mountain shack and find a larger base of operations for a catering business. Patrick and Reinhardt bought a farm just over the mountain, surrounded by Shenandoah National Park and traversed by a river. "It had been an old, self-sufficient homestead with a brandy distillery, a mill, and orchards. It was a perfect, private world. Naturally, I never wanted to leave," he says.

To get by, Patrick mowed grass for neighbors in a 40-mile radius, including James J. Kilpatrick, the columnist. "When his wife found out I cooked, I began doing parties for them—first just washing dishes but pretty soon I did seated dinners for 300. The area was starved for any kind of wholesome and sophisticated food. It was a long way to the nearest grocery store and there were a lot of wealthy people down mile-long driveways who couldn't entertain their guests."

Patrick likes to change the display of plates in the kitchen's glass cases. Each plate has special meaning. "Here's our first restaurant china, a plate from our favorite steak house that burned down, my grandmother's pattern," he says.

Their flourishing catering business was at a crossroads in no time. Patrick and Reinhardt were still cooking at their farm on an old wood-burning stove supplemented with an electric hot plate. Worse, the food had to be carted over a plank across their bridgeless river. "We decided to make them come to us. We decided to have a restaurant."

Twenty dazzling, success-filled years later, Patrick says, "As much as you might try to run away from restaurant work, all sorts of other pursuits seem to pale. I love the tense excitement and the spontaneity of dealing with the public. And then there are those interesting characters the business is so well known for." Indeed.

Above, The inn's kitchen features a showpiece hood designed by Joyce Evans, designer of Patrick's home kitchen. **Left,** Patrick uses his custom-made Vulcan "piano" range to create the restaurant's famous cuisine. "I take the finest local ingredients—simple, earthy, soulful—and combine them in unusual, sometimes startling, ways," he says. Also unusual: the Dalmatian-print kitchen uniforms.

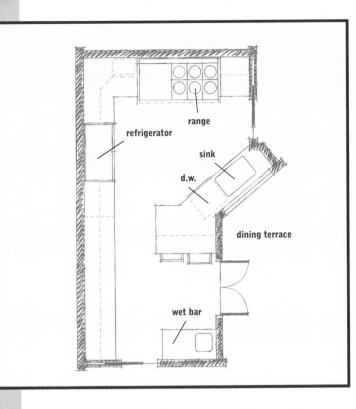

refrigerator

range

sink

d.w.

dining terrace

wet bar

When he started cooking, Alsatian chef Hubert Keller apprenticed with five of the most renowned chefs in France—Haeberlin, Le-Notre, Maximin, Bocuse, and Verge. In San Francisco, Hubert proves he learned well; his top-rated Fleur de Lys restaurant thrills diners with classically in-spired, innovative dishes. In 1996, The Cuisine of Hubert Keller was published; the next year, he received the James Beard Award for Best Chef in California.

Opposite, *Hubert and his wife, Chantal, enjoy cooking together in their handsomely remodeled home kitchen.*

"...from this spot I can do everything. You don't want to have to walk from the stove to the refrigerator. You want to be able to just turn."

Hubert Keller

"Naturally, I wanted to be a pastry chef," says Hubert Keller. His parents ran a *pâtisserie* in Ribeauville in the French Alsace, so what else could he be? However, his culinary training took another route when the father of a friend hired the 16-year-old Hubert as an apprentice in his restaurant. The friend's father was Paul Haeberlin and the restaurant was Auberge de L'Ill—a Michelin three-star establishment.

Over a four-year period Hubert worked every station in the kitchen, learning the skills and adopting the standards of one of the finest restaurants in France. After Auberge de L'Ill, he began a six-year culinary odyssey, working in restaurants from Paris to Provence under the tutelage of four of France's most renowned chefs—Gaston Le-Notre, Jacques Maximin, Paul Bocuse, and Roger Verge. Eventually, Verge asked the newly wed Keller to start up La Cuisine de Soleil in Brazil and, later, the Sutter 500 Restaurant in San Francisco. So Hubert and his wife, Chantal, made the big move, and in 1986, he became chef and co-owner of Fleur de Lys, one of the most widely acclaimed French restaurants in the San Francisco Bay area.

Hubert is well known for his attention to presentation. But presentation apparently was far from the mind of the woman who sold her townhouse to the Kellers. "There were no cookies in the oven," when the Kellers first saw the house, he says. No alluring aromas drifting from the all-important kitchen to entice buyers. Except for its peerless Bay view, charming internal terrace, and large living room, the 1933 house offered few attractions. The kitchen was neglected and stale, with "potato sack" burlap covering the walls. Hubert and Chantal shudder in unison while describing the kitchen curtains, stiff with years of accumulated dirt. Walls segmented the kitchen work areas into a dark, dated warren.

Nevertheless, the kitchen had promise. Without the intruding walls, its size and shape—basically an 11-ft. by 16-ft. rectangle—were good. A skylight was in place. Facing the rear of the house, the kitchen and terrace were impressively quiet. In their minds, the Kellers already envisioned a sparkling, remodeled kitchen. Furthermore, they loved the idea of living by the water. So they

that a separate unit need not take up valuable counter space. The range fan and vent are also professional quality, and the stainless-steel hood was mounted extra high so the 6-ft.-tall Hubert won't bump his head.

The Kellers wanted a "solid, heavy-duty Traulsen, the Rolls Royce of refrigerators," Hubert says. The Traulsen has four compartments that can be set at different temperatures—a practical configuration for storing produce. And, when they're feeling less practical, the Kellers can easily chill 24 bottles of champagne on the top shelf. There is a small separate freezer, an ice maker, and a large ice drawer. Some models have glass doors—convenient for a restaurant setting—but the Kellers didn't want the refrigerator's contents in constant view. Both Franke sinks are stainless steel. The primary sink—in the work triangle—has a pull-out faucet which eliminates struggles to position large pots underneath. A secondary sink is in the wet bar.

Other than the equipment, two requirements shaped the design of the Keller kitchen—a smoothly functional work area and abundant counter space. Basically an open triangle formed by two walls and a broad, angled peninsula, the food preparation area is compact and efficient. "There's plenty of space to move around, bend down, open things up," says Hubert. Cabinet and appliance doors do not collide. All doors to the room are sliders that remain out of the way.

The Miele dishwasher is next to the sink. "The refrigerator, stove, sink, work surfaces—everything is close together," says Hubert. Even if his kitchen were bigger, Hubert says he would keep the work area this compact. "Here you have a very small space, but from this spot I can do everything—you don't want to walk from the stove to the refrigerator to the sink. You want to be able to just turn." In commercial kitchens the stove is far from the refrigerator because of the heat, he says. At home all the work areas are close. Yet, the kitchen has plenty of counter space. "That's why we really like our kitchen," says Chantal. "We actually have more counter space in our small kitchen than we find in many of the mansions where we do catering jobs."

It's not surprising that aesthetics were as important as function in the kitchen's design. Meandering rivers of color in the gleaming,

bought the house. But instead of designing the space, then fitting it with appliances and cabinetry, the Kellers approached their kitchen remodel the other way around. They collected all the key components and stored them in the basement, ready to be installed. Then they built a design around these essentials.

The solid, commercial-grade Armour Wolf range has two ovens, one large and one small. "A huge oven is almost a waste when you're heating up little things," explains Hubert. The larger oven is pressed into service for holidays and parties. Hubert slid the extra-deep appliance into place along the kitchen's back wall. Neatly flush with the kitchen counters, it bulges several inches into a closet behind the room. Six burners and a built-in flattop griddle complete the arrangement. The slot under the griddle doubles as a salamander broiler so

Although they live on blustery San Francisco Bay, the Kellers' open-air, interior terrace provides a protected haven from the elements—and the busy world. Since it connects with the kitchen through double French doors, Hubert and Chantal often enjoy quiet conversation and a luxurious brunch in the sun on their terrace built for two.

the impressive silver duck press—Hubert loves to tell about the "old days" in France, when every restaurant of quality had a full-time *canardier,* the person responsible for pressing the ducks.

Hubert and Chantal also are passionate about their collection of antique pastry molds. On the wall, on ledges, tucked away in cabinets are molds they have collected in Europe and America. Especially nostalgic are the swirl-patterned ceramic *kugelhopf* molds that belonged to Hubert's father. With a smile, Hubert demonstrates that some of the molds still have a characteristic aroma from years of baking the festive holiday cakes of the same name. He also shows how his father would tap the ornate metal chocolate molds with a small wooden stick so that the still-liquid chocolate would form up perfectly.

In San Francisco, the Kellers often spend their Sundays searching antique stores for pastry molds and other culinary treasures to add to their collection. Before setting out, they enjoy a relaxing brunch in the sun on the cozy terrace adjoining the kitchen—*café au lait,* fresh fruits, truffles, scrambled eggs, and, of course, homemade brioche. Standing contentedly in his kitchen, Hubert muses quietly, "Chantal and I were supposed to be here for just six months." Somehow those six months stretched into years.

Those years have brought success and satisfaction to the Kellers. *The Cuisine of Hubert Keller* was published in 1996. In 1997 Hubert received the James Beard Award as Best Chef in California. With Hubert overseeing the kitchen and Chantal handling Fleur de Lys' public relations, the couple have established themselves as top restaurateurs in a demanding "restaurant town."

Fleur de Lys showcases Hubert's classic—but updated and original—French cuisine. He plays upon a mix of tradition and adventure to create such artful dishes as chilled asparagus soup with a

dark Tibetan marble counters form a visual flow between the pale cherry wood cabinets and the ceramic tile floor. The marble is also a durable surface that can withstand very high temperatures. Hubert points proudly to the thin strip of stainless steel inset around the edges of the marble—an aesthetic extra that forms a subtle and pleasing connection to the appliances.

Solid wood cabinet doors conceal cutting boards, utensils, and deep pull-out storage bins for pots and pans. An arrangement of ladles and copper pots softens the expanse of stainless steel at the cooktop. Glass-faced cabinets display fine china and glassware. Cabinetry that steps up the side wall was designed expressly to frame

Left and below, The Kellers had specially designed cabinets constructed for their cooking tools and serving pieces. They have a collection of antique kugelhopf *and chocolate molds—heirlooms from Hubert's father, who was a pastry chef in France.*

timbale of imperial caviar, crabmeat, and avocado; crunchy prawns in salsify accented with Pinot Noir sauce and vanilla oil; and seared Ahi tuna on a fondue of green onions and ginger. It comes as a pleasing bonus that the health-conscious Keller has made light sauces, fresh herbs, and vegetables—particularly root vegetables—integral to his signature dishes. Five-course vegetarian dinners are offered at the restaurant. Desserts are as delicious and elaborate as you would expect from someone who grew up having brioche and fine Easter Bunny-shaped chocolates packed in his school lunch.

After 16 years, San Francisco is home for the Kellers. And when Hubert misses the family *pâtisserie,* he has plenty of marble counter space to make fine pastry right at home in California.

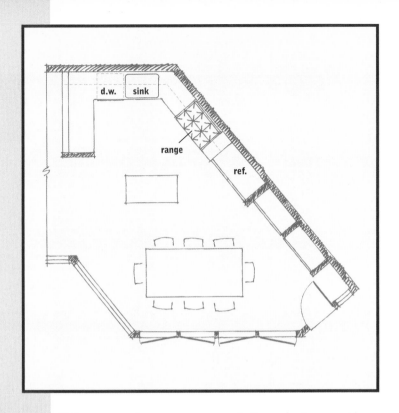

d.w. sink

range

ref.

Border Grill Ciudad

Mary Sue Milliken is co-owner of the award-winning Border Grill in Santa Monica, California, which serves top-notch Mexican food. Ciudad, her newest venture with business partner Susan Feniger, offers Latin cuisine. Mary Sue and Susan star in Too Hot Tamales, *a Food Network TV show, and are the authors of* Cooking with Too Hot Tamales, Cantina, Mesa Mexicana, *and* City Cuisine.

Opposite, *Mary Sue's husband, Josh Schweitzer, designed the stylish, pool-side kitchen.*

"Since my life revolves around food, how the kitchen functions is really important to me. Josh is an architect, so he cares about how things look."

Mary Sue Milliken

Only in L.A. would you find such a wild and wonderful mix: the taller, blond half of the smash cooking duo *Too Hot Tamales* and her husband living in a converted 1950s swimming school. Add two lively boys, Declan, 8, Kieren, 5 months, and a couple of adventuresome dogs named Lewis and Clark, and the result is a house full of hot tamales. And, by design, the family's pool-side kitchen is at the center of it all.

Right, *Mary Sue has an open kitchen, which enables her to cook while staying involved in everything else that is going on in the house. The kitchen space is loosely defined by a "floating," swimming-pool-blue structure overhead.* **Opposite top,** *The compact but efficient work area puts everything close at hand and has a centrally located work island.* **Opposite bottom,** *Knives are neatly compartmentalized in a drawer.*

Mary Sue Milliken, co-owner of the colorful Border Grill in Santa Monica and Ciudad in downtown Los Angeles—and co-star of cable TV's *Too Hot Tamales* cooking show—along with her husband, Josh Schweitzer, who is an architect in L.A., bought the old west-side neighborhood swimming school in 1985. Although both fell in love with the idea of living alongside a giant swimming pool, the building, with its little snack bar and banks of toilets and shower stalls, was clearly not suited for round-the-clock living.

In short order, they targeted areas for demolition. Walls between the former snack bar and men's locker room came down to create space for an open, California-style kitchen and dining area adjoining the pool. But once the space was opened up, the couple ran low on money. "We tore out everything except for one toilet and a shower out by the pool," Mary Sue remembers. "We moved in and lived like that for five years, with just an outdoor shower."

By the time the couple moved ahead with their remodel they knew they wanted a free-flowing, clean-looking living space that

Cabinet tops display art and treasures gathered on trips to exotic locales. Josh designed the handsome, clean-lined cabinets with flip-up opening mechanisms so that they have no visible hardware.

integrated the pool and highlighted the kitchen; but there were a few stumbling blocks. Mary Sue explains, "Since my life revolves around food, how the kitchen functions is really important to me, but that's not as important to Josh. He's an architect, so he cares about how things look." Mary Sue always wanted the kitchen open, "really open—open to the rest of the living space, inside and out." That way she can cook *and* stay involved with whatever is going on.

"When you have people over, everybody ends up in the kitchen. And since we only have about 800 sq. ft. downstairs, I wanted the kitchen to be part of one big room, rather than having everybody crowding into a tiny space.

"However, Josh kept designing things, like full-height walls or a special little pantry for the refrigerator. He wanted things hidden away, but I kept going over the plans and exposing and opening up again. In the end, we compromised."

The result is a pleasing combination of open living space and a small but stylish kitchen with sleek, compact cabinets that look good from every angle. Josh designed the overhead cabinet doors with a "flip up" opening mechanism to enhance their streamlined look—there's no visible hardware such as hinges or knobs. "We don't need much storage because I don't have many gadgets for cooking," she says. "And then, to please Josh, we put things away when we're not using them, so I try to keep equipment to a minimum."

The cabinets form a display area for art and treasures from Mary Sue and Josh's travels. Lights were installed on the cabinet tops to highlight their collections of photographs, rustic pottery, model sailboats, and exotic wood carvings, while under-cabinet lighting floods the countertops. The kitchen space is defined by a floating, light-blue structure that contains an extra-large, round fluorescent light to give off an underwater feel. Tranquil tones of green and blue wash the kitchen and connect it visually with the swimming pool through the wood-framed glass walls and doors that replaced a cement block wall.

Josh also designed a small, streamlined island with a chopping-block top and storage underneath. The island is strategically placed between the kitchen and the dining table so Mary Sue can work, look out to the pool, and talk to everyone at the table. The dining room table and chairs, again designed by Josh, are clean, modernistic, and finished in soft colors.

As for equipment and appliances, Mary Sue loves her extra-deep, stainless-steel trough sink for washing giant pots and pans (she wishes the sink had a view, however). A Dacor oven, vent, and five-burner cooktop passed Josh's "sleekness" test, and Mary Sue approves of the high BTUs it generates. She prizes her KitchenAid refrigerator because the freezer is on bottom. "I don't use the freezer much, so why have it at eye level? Instead you should have the refrigerator up there, because you're constantly in the refrigerator, looking for things." The couple's KitchenAid WhisperQuiet dishwasher lives up to its name, an important consideration when the kitchen is open to the living areas.

Mary Sue appreciates her maple countertops because the hardwood holds up to heavy use. "I really beat the heck out of them. At

Left, *Cabinets are designed to hold delicate stemware.*

Above, *Two large pantry closets store colorful, retro dishes and serving pieces.*

Above left, The upper cabinets store spices for ready access at the cooktop. *Above right,* Proof positive that cabinets do not need to look bulky. Mary Sue rubs her maple countertops weekly with mineral oil to keep them looking good.

Thanksgiving I take my turkey right out of the oven and slap it down on the counter for carving." As long as the counters are rubbed once a week with mineral oil, they hold up just fine. "If you don't treat them with oil," Mary Sue warns, "they mildew or get dried out and they look really awful." If she had it to do over, she would have installed an under-mounted sink with the counter extending over the edge of the sink to make it easier to wipe the counters clean.

Recently, Mary Sue added a second-floor home office overlooking the pool, so that she has the option of working from home until the baby is older. Mary Sue and her business partner, Susan Feniger—the shorter, brunette "Hot Tamale"—divide their many responsibilities: Mary Sue concentrates on cookbooks, television, and radio work; Susan handles the restaurants. The two met 20 years ago as recent chef school graduates working in the kitchen of the haute cuisine Le Perroquet in Chicago. After that, France was their next choice for additional culinary education. Mary Sue headed to Restaurant d'Olympe in Paris and Susan to the kitchen of L'Oasis on the Riviera.

Once back home in 1981, they launched the tiny City Café on Melrose Avenue in L.A. City Café was followed by CITY, an urbane, much larger restaurant whose eclectic menu was guided by the pair's formal French training but that served spicy, robust foods influenced by travels to Thailand, India, and Mexico. Border Grill, named one of the best restaurants in America by *Gourmet* magazine, opened in 1985. It continues to serve up what *Los Angeles* magazine called "arguably the most serious Mexican food in town," featuring luscious green corn tamales and sautéed rock shrimp with *ancho* chiles. Now Ciudad has joined the Milliken-Feniger stable, serving a wide variety of Latin foods from South America, Central America, Spain, and Portugal.

Both Mary Sue and Susan played a founding role in Women Chefs and Restaurateurs, which fosters the careers of women in restaurants, and in Chefs Collaborative 2000, which advocates the use of sustainably grown products in the food service industry. Mary Sue says, "It's very clear when you're a chef that the product is really what makes the difference. It's not us so much that we are working the magic. It's the product that is already magical when it comes out of the ground—or at least it should be."

In her personal life, Mary Sue is likewise committed to sustainable agriculture. She belongs to a CSA (community-supported agriculture) produce co-op through which she receives a weekly "mystery" bag of seasonal fruits and vegetables grown on a small, local farm. Mary

Left, *The oversized dining table and colorful chairs, designed by Josh, are strategically placed between kitchen and palm-fringed swimming pool—a great spot for 5-month-old Kieren to taste his first solid food.* **Below,** *The kitchen looks out to the pool through floor-to-ceiling glass doors and windows, which took the place of a concrete block wall. Mary Sue calls the remodeled home her "oasis."*

Sue says, "My menus at home are based on what I get from the CSA. I might get a whole flat of peaches, so we'll eat a lot of cobblers, or I'll get a huge bag of assorted root vegetables; then I love to make a lentil stew with kohlrabi, turnips, parsnip, and celery root in it."

The family's favorite meal is basmati rice and yellow split peas "with tons of garlic and onions and basil." They also like giant salads with tuna, eggs, and son Declan's special croutons. When it's Josh's turn to cook, the most likely menu is chili and cornbread.

Coming from a "staunchly German" family on her mother's side, food was important in Mary Sue's childhood Michigan home. "My Mom was a great, traditional cook and superb baker, but she also loved to learn new kinds of cooking from all over the world." The family's habit was to sit down and have dinner, then "a couple of us would get up and wash the dishes while everybody else sat around and got into heated political arguments or solved the problems of the world. It was definitely a 'lingering' sort of thing. My sisters and I loved it."

At night, Mary Sue, Josh, and the children continue the good food and tradition of lingering around their dinner table. Mary Sue calls their home an oasis, and certainly the palm-fringed pool fits the classic definition of a "green spot in the desert, made so by the presence of water." But, she also means that her home is a secluded retreat, "protected, relaxing, and pleasing"—a true home, with a wonderful kitchen, improbably carved from an old swimming school.

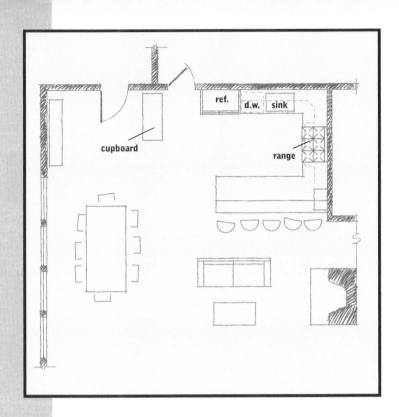

cupboard

ref. d.w. sink

range

"We liked the idea of the kitchen being integral to the living space—dinner parties are fun because once guests are in our home, they're also in the kitchen."

Charles Dale

Renaissance

Charles Dale trained with chefs Daniel Boulud, Alain Sailhac, and Barry Wine. In 1990, he opened Renaissance, his award-winning restaurant in Aspen, Colorado; the "R" Bistro is upstairs. In 1998, Charles was a James Beard Award Nominee for Best Chef in the Southwest. Food & Wine magazine named him one of the Best New Chefs in America in 1995. With his wife, Aimée, Charles wrote The Chefs' Guide to America's Best Restaurants. He developed a line of marinades for the St. Dalfour label.

Opposite, Charles and Aimée enjoy making cookies.

Returning home late one night from his Aspen, Colorado, restaurant, Charles Dale was astonished to find that a large bear had broken into the garage and was eating its way through several cases of his savory, imported marinades. Though only a 12-minute drive from Renaissance, Charles' elegant downtown dining establishment, "it's nature out here—elk, cottontail rabbits, porcupines, deer, fox, marmot, bears, you name it," he says. Charles and his wife, Aimée, had moved from town so they could have animals, but this wasn't exactly what they had in mind.

The newly wed Dales found their appealing mountain home near Aspen in 1997. After living in the area for 10 years, Charles wanted a house with views and a kitchen that would be suitable for entertaining and for his popular cooking classes. Aimée was focusing on room for the dogs and horses she could own. Spectacular vistas and lots of wide-open spaces came with the house, but the kitchen needed a full-fledged equipment update.

The 1970s kitchen, a compact, U-shaped work area in one corner of an expansive living space, boasted a broad, comfortable eating bar, dark gray-green marble tile countertops, and maple cabinets that were worth saving. However, the appliances were not up to standard. "The old kitchen had a very strange electric range," Charles recalls. "Only four burners, but with double ovens—something I'd never seen before." Although the range was relegated to the used-appliance store, it left a 42-in. opening in the cabinetry, enough space for a six-burner Viking range.

The range had to be converted to propane because there is no gas supply in the Dales' rural area. They also had to consider Aspen's sky-high location. "I like lots of cooking fire power," Charles explains, "and here at altitude you've got a problem—the BTUs are actually lower." So Charles selected a super-charged 22,000-BTU per burner range that ends up delivering a very satisfactory 17,000

BTUs. The "dual fuel" (propane and electric) range has an extra-wide electric oven featuring eight cooking options for maximum flexibility. With four heavy-duty racks, the single, large oven has ample capacity to handle dinner parties or Charles' cooking classes. The range has a high stainless-steel backsplash topped with a shelf that's handy for storing salt and pepper or for use as a warming shelf.

Charles removed the old microwave above the range to create space for the Viking hood. Other Viking equipment includes an ultra-quiet dishwasher and a refrigerator that Charles calls "quite spacious": It has four climate zones and an automatic ice maker.

"We chose the Kohler sink because its main basin works for large pots and cutting boards. It's even big enough for half-sheet pans," Charles says. "That's important. Always buy your sink based on what you're going to do with it."

Other features in the kitchen include a range-side rack for utensils and a stylish, stainless-steel Italian dish drainer, designed to hang over the sink to free up counter space. Every inch of the eating counter is put to use when Charles leads his classes. He says it works perfectly for him to be in the kitchen, working and demonstrating, while students sit on the stools "outside" the kitchen, each with an individual cutting board.

A consistent look was important, too, chiefly because the kitchen is part of the "great room," where Charles and Aimée spend much of their time, eating, listening to music, reading, and admiring the mountain view. Charles says, "When we first saw the house, we liked the idea of the kitchen really being integral to the living space—dinner parties are so much fun because once guests are in our home, they're also in the kitchen." The couple chose warm, honey-colored wood for the hutch, stools, and dining furniture to coordinate with the kitchen cabinets and maple flooring. Because the kitchen is completely open, Aimée keeps it neat and uncluttered. "But then Charles comes in," she says, "and suddenly there are papers everywhere. That's when I say, 'Go to your office.'"

To create an informal entrance area, Charles and Aimée positioned an antique pine hutch between the kitchen and the front door. "The hutch also solved some of our storage problems, " Aimée says. "We received a tremendous amount of plates and glassware when we married."

Charles' earliest food memories are set in Monaco, where his father was Prince Rainier's privy counselor in charge of the country's economic development. Charles remembers working with his family's cook, when he was about five years old, making ravioli. "It was a little kitchen," he says, "but there was an open space with a table where she'd roll out the dough, prepare the filling, then put it all together by hand. It's a very crystalline memory for me."

Other favorite childhood foods were braised endive and ham with *béchamel* sauce, sweetbreads, and a specialty from the Riviera called *tourte aux blettes.* Charles says, "I do a version of it in the restaurant, with an almond crust filled with Swiss chard and chanterelle mushrooms, served with a beet sauce." On the other end of the food spectrum, Charles occasionally dared raw onion sandwiches on white bread with mustard—a favorite of his father's—and loved the peanut butter brought back to Monaco from the United States by Princess Grace for her children. During his early years, Charles was schooled in the Royal Palace with Prince Albert and Princess Caroline.

When Charles was seven, the family moved to the Bahamas. Though finding himself in something of a "culinary wasteland" after Monaco, Charles was introduced to every conceivable kind of fish, as well as Jamaican Creole dishes, curries, and "jerked" meats. His culinary odyssey did not stop there. After moving to New York,

Left, A stainless-steel dish drainer hangs over the sink. ***Above,***
The new six-burner range fit into the space left by the old oven.

Charles sampled that city's vast array of ethnic restaurants. Later, as a student at Princeton University, he had international roommates who loved to cook specialties from their homelands. "Food was always central to my life, I just never thought I'd be doing it professionally, " Charles says.

After college, Charles had visions of "making it" as a rock-and-roll musician, but his band didn't take off. After a few years, he decided "that I'd eat more often and certainly better if I were a chef, not a guitarist." Through a friend Charles managed to get an apprenticeship at Manhattan's Le Cirque, under Alain Sailhac. He also worked with George Mazraff at Paris' Au Quai des Ormes, and, back in New York, as a line cook under Daniel Boulud at the Hotel Plaza Athénée. Next came stints at Barry Wine's Casual Quilted Giraffe and at Léon de Lyon in France, working with Jean-Paul Lacombe. Then Charles was called back to Le Cirque to work again with Boulud, who had taken over as executive chef. By this time, he was "sold" on a culinary career.

"Cooking is a great combination of talents. It's a lot like song writing or playing an instrument. It's a performance. And I'd always wanted to be a troubadour, going around playing my music for people," Charles says. "As it turns out, I get to do that. I travel a fair amount for cooking. Now I'm a culinary troubadour."

While on a ski vacation in 1988, Charles decided that Aspen would be a good place to start a restaurant, have "some fun," and call home. He landed a position as executive sous-chef at the Hotel Jerome and later ran a catering company. In 1990, Charles opened his exclusive, 50-seat Renaissance. It took awhile for the romantic, peach-colored dining room to catch on with the active, outdoorsy crowd, but after a few years Renaissance had become the "in" place for locals, skiers, and celebrities to enjoy an elegant dinner.

The restaurant serves Charles' light, flavorful "modern French" food blended with the hearty but healthful "Alpine" cuisine made with local ingredients. Renaissance features such dishes as braised pheasant in a blue-corn crepe with sun-dried cherry shiraz marmalade, grilled marinated loin of venison with parsnip purée, honeyed chestnuts and chunky applesauce, or crispy Chilean sea bass with artichokes, shiitakes, and foie gras.

Following local custom, Renaissance is open just eight and a half months a year. During down time in spring and fall, Charles and his staff are able "to be off completely, to travel and to refresh our creativity. In this business you have to be happy because you're trying to make other people happy." Charles also has used the time to cook on cruise liners and to work on *The Chefs' Guide to America's Best Restaurants,* which he wrote with Aimée.

In the future, Charles thinks high-quality prepared foods will be a strong trend. He also predicts that people will cook more simply, as their living quarters shrink, and that "we'll do more one-pot meals—an old way of cooking. Last night we made a roast chicken and everything was in there—carrots, mushrooms, onions, potatoes. It's so easy."

For his personal future, Charles would like to do more teaching, possibly on TV, because "I'd like to reach more people than I can in a 50-seat restaurant in Aspen." Obviously, he's reaching quite a few people already: in 1998 he was a James Beard Award Nominee for Best Chef in the Southwest. *Food & Wine* magazine named Charles one of the Best New Chefs in America in 1995. Charles is working on a cookbook and wants to create more food products, like the all-natural marinades he developed. One thing is certain: He won't store them in the garage.

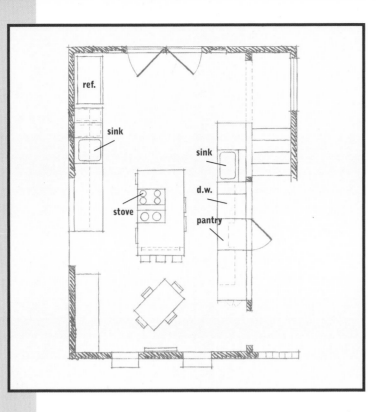

Frontera Grill
Topolobampo

While traveling after college, Rick discovered the richness and complexity of Mexican food and decided to devote his career to the mastery of the cuisine. Winning the James Beard Award for Chef of the Year in 1995 was official recognition that he had done just that. His books include Authentic Mexican: Regional Cooking from the Heart of Mexico *and* Rick Bayless's Mexican Kitchen.

Opposite, *Rick and Deann Bayless' wildly popular restaurants serve authentic Mexican cuisine, but at home their kitchen speaks of the history of Chicago.*

"From the time I was a kid, I was constantly in the kitchen…. It has just been my way of creatively expressing myself."

Rick Bayless

Rick Bayless sees opportunities in unlikely places. For instance, realizing that a gourmet Mexican restaurant could be a hit in the heartland, or that an old neighborhood tavern could be transformed into a family home. Rick and his wife, Deann, had the vision—and the energy—to do both. Within a few years they created Frontera Grill and Topolobampo, two perpetually packed restaurants that serve fine Mexican cuisine to a savvy clientele in Chicago's River North district. And sensing another pearl in the oyster, the Baylesses remodeled the turn-of-the-century "Polly's Polka Palace" to create a sophisticated city residence for themselves and their eight-year-old daughter, Lanie.

Pine cabinets and iron hardware add to a turn-of-the-century ambiance, **opposite.** Rick's garden, **below,** feeds the family and attests to his commitment to sustainable agriculture. The Beard Foundation recently awarded him its Humanitarian Award for establishing Chefs Collaborative 2000—a network devoted to supplying restaurants with locally grown produce.

Most house hunters would have crossed the building off their list and hit the gas after one look at the beer sign that still swings outside the door of the old neighborhood tavern. But behind the bland brick facade and corner-bar ambiance Rick and Deann realized a magical space—a quiet, very private retreat that embraces original features of the 1916 building and blends them with their own sense of style.

At the end of the living room, and up two steps, is Polly's former barroom, now the kitchen, a simple but generous 14-ft. by 23-ft. rectangle stretching across the back of the house. Rick and Deann designed the layout to be straightforward and practical, with distinct areas for food preparation and cleanup. Previous owners, who began the conversion from tavern to home, had refurbished the kitchen, but it wasn't what Rick and Deann had in mind.

While planning the remodel, the Baylesses found that most of their decisions were based on the desire for a no-nonsense, functional kitchen. But good looks mattered, too, and it was important for the new room to harmonize with the turn-of-the-century house. Finally, the space had to be suitable for the television work and cooking classes that are part of Rick's everyday life.

On the practical side, generously sized, durable counters were a must for Rick. "We knew we wanted rock," but without the more for-

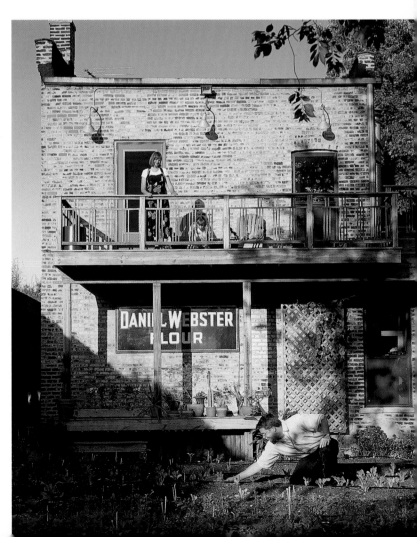

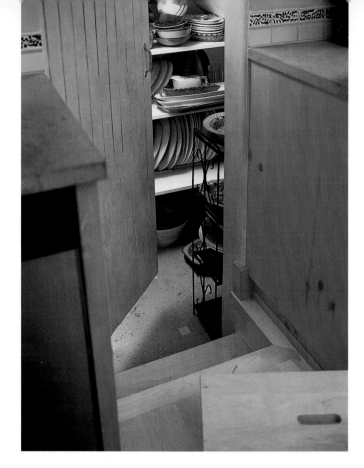

Above, A dish pantry makes good use of space under the second-story back stairs. The pull-out block conceals two stairs and doubles as Lanie's step stool. ***Opposite,*** After the remodel was finished Rick insisted on buying a "funky, old, weather-beaten 'Pueblo Deco' style table and chairs," to take the new edge off the space. Greenhouse windows bring light into the kitchen. Deann's favorite whimsical collages are by Mexican artist Rodolfo Morales.

mal look of marble or granite, says Rick. As they began investigating options, they discovered and fell in love with the well-worn patina of an old soapstone sink. Rick learned that such sinks were still being made in Vermont and that slabs of soapstone would make solid countertops. The search was over: The two dark gray soapstone apron sinks and smooth, matte-finish counters are a literal "cornerstone" of the new kitchen.

To carry out their idea of separate cleanup and prep spaces, Rick and Deann stationed the refrigerator on one side of the room, a step away from the vegetable sink and chopping areas. Opposite, the deep trough sink, under-counter dishwasher, and pantry tucked under the back stairs make for easy cleanup and storage of tableware. In the middle of the room, the chef placed a large maple chopping block island, which houses his commercial-grade Five Star range.

The biggest design challenge was venting the Five Star. Because the Baylesses did not want to cut into the old pressed-tin ceiling to install a hood and vent, they dropped a heavy-duty down-draft system right into the island. The unobtrusive, 8-in.-high unit can be lowered out of sight when it's not needed, and its powerful exhaust system, customized by Viking, works so well that Rick added a small grill.

The range has a small gas oven, an electric convection oven for baking, and six burners plus a large griddle, "because cooking on the griddle is common in Mexican cuisine," Rick says. He likes using heavy iron or copper skillets to achieve even heat and also likes the weight of LeCreuset cookware. Rick stores some pots in deep drawers next to the range. Others hang on a rack by the cleanup sink.

Floor-to-ceiling doors at the east end of the kitchen and greenhouse windows at the other end fill the kitchen with natural light dur-

ing the day. To keep the electric lighting in character with the old house (Polly's was built in the gas-light era, and the old tavern still had holes in the ceiling for lamps), Rick installed electrified billiard lamps covered with their original glass globes. Elsewhere, unobtrusive, super-thin (½ in.) lights recessed into the bases of the wall cabinets light countertops. Low-voltage interior cabinet lights cast a warm glow over the glassware and Mexican crockery.

During the remodel, Rick and Deann considered air-conditioning but found the price too steep. Instead, they agreed to focus on the allure of a backyard flower garden with a large water feature that tempts them outside whenever the kitchen gets too hot. Just beyond the flowers, a 1,000-sq.-ft. kitchen garden provides seasonal produce for home and restaurant. Considering Rick's commitment to fostering sustainable agriculture through "buying from farmers down the road," it seems natural that he would dig in and grow a few vegetables right in his own backyard.

For additional heat during the long Chicago winters, low-profile radiator panels recess into the outer walls of the kitchen and into the

ends of the island, where they are camouflaged so well that they are barely noticeable.

Yet even after the remodeling, Rick felt that the kitchen was incomplete. A self-professed "antiques person," he disliked the unrelenting newness of his kitchen, so he went out and bought a "funky, old, weather-beaten 'Pueblo Deco' style table and chairs" to take the pristine edge off the space. The Baylesses gather around that table every day for a family breakfast before Lanie goes to school, after which Rick and Deann prepare for the evening's presentations at Frontera and Topolobampo.

Even as a boy growing up in Oklahoma City, Rick enjoyed the pleasures of cooking and sharing good food. His grandmother was a great cook, and he loved to watch her work. He also watched with admiration as his parents worked side by side to serve up savory, slow-smoke barbecue at their Hickory House restaurant.

"From the time I was a kid, I was constantly in the kitchen. I was always whipping up special meals," Rick says. "It has just been my way of creatively expressing myself." Those cooking skills supported him while he earned a degree in Spanish language and Latin American culture, followed by a master's degree in linguistics. After graduate school, Rick found a way to combine his interests in cooking, Latin American culture, language, and research: He and Deann went to Mexico to investigate the country's regional cuisines firsthand.

After living in Mexico for seven years (interspersed with stints as a chef in Los Angeles and Cleveland) Rick had become an enthusiastic and well-versed proponent of true Mexican cuisine. Searching for a city that hadn't already been saturated with anglicized Mexican cooking and where diners would be adventurous and discriminating enough to taste and appreciate "real" Mexican cuisine, they settled on Chicago. In 1987 they opened the colorful and casual Frontera Grill, followed two years later by the fine-dining Topolobampo next door.

While Deann manages the floor, Rick creates the menus and runs the kitchen for both restaurants. Topolobampo features such dishes as Pato a la Naranja (Amish country duck with orangey, sweet-sour *ancho* chile sauce, served with mashed Mexican pumpkin) and Mone de Dorado (garlic-marinated Gulf mahimahi baked in banana leaves with aromatic hoja santa, ripe tomatoes, *güero* chile, and sweet plantains, served with seared serrano salsa). Frontera's menu is just as exotic and appealing.

In 1995 Rick won the James Beard Award for Chef of the Year, the first winner to specialize in a non-European cuisine. A few years later he received the James Beard Humanitarian Award for his work to establish Chefs Collaborative 2000, an organization that promotes sustainable agriculture. Squeezing out a little more time from his schedule, Rick markets a line of Frontera salsas—"flavors born of

Opposite, Rick and Deann's treasured collection of colorful Mexican cazuelas *and* ollas glows warmly atop their kitchen bookshelves. **Left,** Dark gray soapstone sinks and countertops make durable, handsome work surfaces that are in keeping with the 90-year-old house. An extra-deep apron sink with adjustable faucet is ideal for washing even the largest pots and pans with ease. Rick prefers his pots hung against a wall and out of the way, rather than on an overhead rack. He cites a fondness for heavy, cast-iron cookware because it spreads the heat so evenly.

the fire," he calls them. And he's written two books, *Authentic Mexican: Regional Cooking from the Heart of Mexico* and *Rick Bayless's Mexican Kitchen,* which he wrote with Deann and Jean Marie Brownson.

Rick dedicated his first book to his grandmother. When it came time to set up his own household, he knew that he wanted a family kitchen like his grandmother's—a warm and welcoming space where he, Deann, and Lanie could gather to cook, eat, and relax. In their newly remodeled former tavern, they have it.

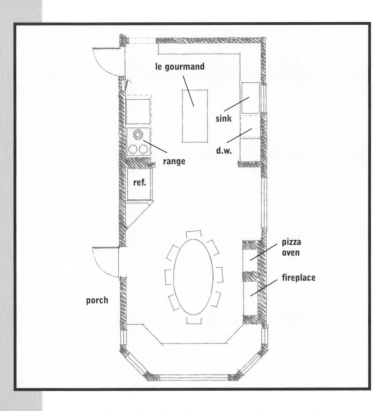

Labels in floor plan: le gourmand, sink, range, d.w., ref., porch, pizza oven, fireplace

"It's important that kids know where their food comes from, that they learn how to take care of the land, and that they take pleasure at the table."

Alice Waters

Chez Panisse
Café Fanny

Alice Waters opened Chez Panisse in 1971, pioneering what she calls "Market Cuisine." She also devotes time to community-based food and vegetable gardening projects. Her cookbooks include The Chez Panisse Menu Cookbook _and_ Chez Panisse Vegetables. _Alice's accolades include Chef of the Year and Restaurant of the Year, both awarded by the Beard Foundation in 1992._

Opposite, _Alice's home kitchen reflects her love of French country cooking, from its La Cornue range to the well-used chopping block table and copper sink._

When Alice Waters first peeked into the house she eventually bought, she was crushed to see that the kitchen was the size of a shoebox.

For the owner of Chez Panisse, one of the country's premier restaurants, a generous kitchen and eating area was essential. The quaint, wisteria-covered Victorian bungalow had other excellent features: beautifully crafted interior woodwork, 10-ft. ceilings, and lots of windows that reach out from bays. And it wasn't far from Chez Panisse. The decision to buy the house and remodel the kitchen was easy; Alice knows good raw material when she sees it.

The tiny, four-square kitchen (less than 12 ft. on a side) and dilap-idated back porch were instantly transformed—in her mind, at least—into a large, open, congenial room where family and friends could cook and eat together. The only other requirement was a wood-burning fireplace and pizza oven.

Alice first added a 20-ft. by 12-ft. dining area to the kitchen. Craftsman touches such as boxed beams and finely trimmed case-ment windows helped integrate the new with the old. To further age the look of the space, Alice moved an Art Nouveau stained-glass win-dow and a carved wood door from the front of the house to the addi-tion. The kitchen retained its original U-shaped layout, with a sink under the window opposite the stove and refrigerator, and glass-front built-in cabinets along the connecting wall. An extra-heavy butcher block island with storage underneath completed the arrangement.

With the "bones" of the kitchen in place, Alice began to refine the details. She knew she wanted a timeless, old-world ambiance for the kitchen—Provence, rather than California—with plenty of space for hand-preparing fresh food. Alice has no great love for elaborate kitchen equipment and when asked to characterize her cooking is apt to say, "non-electric." Her straightforward kitchen philosophy centers on involvement with food through all the senses—not just smell and taste—so that hand-crushing garlic is far more instructive and satisfying to the cook than grinding it in a food processor; Alice's mortar and pestle is her favorite kitchen tool.

Instead of gleaming, high-tech equipment, Alice relies on basic tools: sharp knives, simple copper pots, and iron skillets. "I have three different sizes of skillets, which I use much more than all those sauté pans," she says. Alice also has a lot of heavy copper with

*The focal point of the kitchen is the brick cook-in fireplace and pizza oven, **opposite,** where Alice roasts meats on the rotisserie, grills vegetables, or bakes pizza. In winter, the fireplace is used daily and sets the scene for cozy gatherings around an oval table. The butcher block table, **left,** allows several cooks to work together and provides convenient storage for pots and pans. Alice values her custom-made copper trough sink, **above,** because it's deep enough for big pots or bowls and is reflective without being shiny.*

stainless-steel lining. "Except for the iron cookware, I insist on cookware that doesn't react with foods, so I don't use tin-lined copper. Iron cookware does react with food, but the extra iron you get with your meal is beneficial."

Because she dislikes the modern look of stainless steel, Alice had copper panels made to slip on the front of her Sub-Zero refrigerator. More copper shows up in the custom-made, extra-deep trough sink. "I love to work in this sink, washing vegetables or salad, because it's both reflective and very warm looking," says Alice. The copper gets a nice patina and "you can either polish it or not," depending on your taste or mood. But, she adds smiling, "if you polish it, then over about a week it just gets nicely patinated again. I actually prefer materials that show wear when you use them." The faucet swings and is mounted high enough so that large pots or bowls fit underneath with ease.

A small, galvanized bucket sits beside the sink for vegetable scraps that are composted daily. Alice's unqualified commitment to reuse and recycle means that other containers are close at

Although it has worked flaw-lessly since it was custom-built, the fireplace wasn't always beautiful in Alice's eyes. Originally constructed of new brick, it didn't have the patina of age and use that its owner thought would look best in her kitchen. One day, a friend suggested rubbing thinned-down paint on the bricks and mortar. The "miraculous" result is a fire-place that now works—and looks—just the way Alice always wanted.

hand in her kitchen—there's even a cloth tote for collecting plastic produce bags.

The canary yellow La Cornue stove is not merely a beautiful object in the kitchen. This ultra-expensive and hard-working French range has a vaulted oven that ensures a consistent flow of very hot, humid air, so food retains its fresh flavor and browns beautifully. The cook-top has two conventional gas burners and a *plaque coup de feu*—a solid cast iron surface that provides graduated heat; the chef can move her skillet around on it rather than constantly adjusting the temperature with a knob. Because Alice doesn't like hoods and fans, she built the vent hood into a wall behind the stove—in the French style—and placed the vent motor in the attic. With the motor so far away, the venting action is virtually silent.

Behind the stove, on countertops and backsplashes, Alice used African slate tiles. They are a stunning mix of grays, black, greens, rust, and browns that are naturally varied in color. Alice thinks they're "absolutely great, because if you spill oil or anything on them, you can just rub it in."

She chose oak for the floors: "I wanted a floor that wasn't cold, that I could walk on without shoes." To cut down on maintenance, the floors were stained with an aniline dye—a soft, olive green color Alice loves. "Those tinted floors do age nicely, but you still have to maintain them," she says. The lower-maintenance African slate might have been a good choice for the kitchen floor as well, she says, except she wanted the underfoot warmth of wood flooring.

The room's *pièce de résistance* is a large, brick cook-in fireplace. At waist level, the open fireplace has a Tuscan grill and a rotisserie for meat. Folding metal doors can be closed if the fireplace is cold. When Alice finishes cooking, the ashes fall to a lower compartment for easy collection; the hot ash pile can be used to cook truffles or potatoes. Eventually, the ashes are spread in a backyard vegetable garden. Alice uses her fireplace continually in winter, for everything from grilling fresh vegetables to making toast. At one side of the fire-place is a wood-burning oven for baking bread or pizza. Everything cooked in the oven has a delicious smoky flavor that family and friends love.

Below, Homemade vinegars age in barrels that fit underneath Alice's butcher block table. The oak floor was washed with a light green aniline dye to give it a soft color. *Right,* Alice displays traditional French café au lait bowls and other pottery in a built-in corner cabinet. The same bowls are used at Café Fanny, Alice's breakfast and lunch restaurant named after her daughter.

Although it's worked flawlessly since day one, the fireplace wasn't always beautiful in Alice's eyes. Because she and the mason were neophytes—not many wood-burning pizza ovens had been built in this country back in 1982—the building process was rocky. As the mason became frustrated with Alice's changes and suggestions, he would end their daily consultations by warning, "If you don't know by tomorrow, I'll go." Finally, she told the mason to go ahead and build it. He did—out of new brick. Alice didn't have the stamina to start over, but she didn't like the modern brick's look either. She says, "I struggled with that new brick for years."

Alice spends time in the Edible Schoolyard at Berkeley's Martin Luther King, Jr., Middle School. The project involves children in planting, gardening, harvesting, cooking, and eating food. The goal: to illuminate the vital relationship of food to their lives while teaching them respect for each other and the planet.

Then one day last summer, Alice says, "my friend was painting the walls in the kitchen and, listening to my fireplace lament, she said, 'Well, you know, we can just rub paint on it and age it a hundred years.' So, she did—just thinned down the paint and rubbed it in. It's a miracle. Suddenly it looked like it had been there forever—it's perfect."

A corner cupboard across from the fireplace holds a handsome collection of *café au lait* bowls—some bought by Alice, others given by friends over the years. These traditional French coffee bowls are also used at Café Fanny, Alice's breakfast and lunch spot she named after her teenage daughter.

While a student at the University of California at Berkeley in the 1960s, Alice took a year of study abroad. In her *Chez Panisse Menu Cookbook,* she describes this experience as a year of eating her way through France—discovering new foods, learning the importance of fresh, well-grown ingredients, and devoting entire days to deciding what and where to eat. She says that trip was the genesis of her "mission" to start a restaurant where she could gather with friends to enjoy fresh, seasonal foods; a mission that culminated in *The New York Times* crediting her with "single-handedly changing the American palate, inspiring a devotion to seasonal cooking and emphasizing the importance of local farmers' markets all over the country."

In France she also learned that communication and conviviality around the dinner table are as important as the meal. Her own slate-topped dining room table seats 12 people in a charmingly eclectic collection of antique wood and tooled-leather chairs. Alice especially values the table's narrow, oval shape, which puts people closer together and encourages lively mealtime conversation.

Sometimes the family uses the butcher block table for meals, and Fanny likes to hang out there for after-school snacks. But Alice wishes the table had a bigger overhang so it would be more comfortable to sit at. Another change she'd make is to add a pantry. "One thing I'm missing here is a nice pantry—I love walk-in storage areas." If she had one, Alice says she would use it to store her vinegar-making barrels, now housed under the butcher block table.

A feature that didn't pan out as planned is the baking center under the garden windows. She installed open shelves for equipment and added pastry marbles and special bins for flour and other ingredients. But "it never happened. I've never really used it. Our local bakery is just too darn close and too good." Instead, the shelves display a treasury of oversized, painted Mexican plates.

In the midst of an urban environment, the Edible Schoolyard reconnects kids to the land and to the pleasure and responsibility of growing their own food. The direct connection between garden and table is also at the heart of Chez Panisse, where Alice relies on and supports her network of local organic-food suppliers.

Alice eagerly shares her vision for the next century of home cooking. "I hope it will be pretty much the same as I've been doing, which is buying organic foods from the farmers' markets, knowing where your food comes from, and growing more in the backyard." Her philosophy is echoed in the Edible Schoolyard, a Berkeley middle-school vegetable gardening and food project gaining national attention.

The garden began when Alice criticized the derelict state of a local school's playground, and the principal subsequently invited her to do something about it. She did—marshaling resources and volunteers to help the children create and sustain an organic garden that's integrated into the school's curriculum and lunch program. "It's terribly important that kids know where their food comes from, that they learn how to take care of the land and how to feed themselves, and that they take pleasure at the table. All these things help build our culture," Alice states. It's easy to see why Alice was named Humanitarian of the Year in 1997 by the James Beard Foundation as a result of her work with such projects as the Edible Schoolyard.

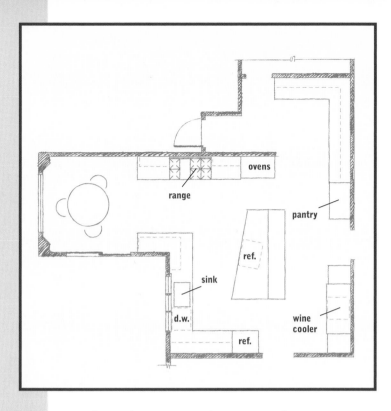

labels in floor plan: ovens, range, pantry, ref., sink, wine cooler, d.w., ref.

Le Bec-Fin
Brasserie
Perrier

Since Georges Perrier's Le Bec-Fin opened in Philadelphia in 1970, it has repeatedly received five-star ratings from the Mobil Travel Guide. *The restaurant garnered* Gourmet's Top Table *designation and, in 1994, was named the Top Restaurant in the United States by* Conde Nast Traveler. *Georges began cooking in France, with several Michelin three-star apprenticeships. He is a member of Maîtres Cuisiniers de France.* Georges Perrier: Le Bec-Fin Recipes *came out in 1997.*

***Opposite,** Georges prepares for an evening's fund-raiser.*

"Lighting may be the room's most important feature. If I told you how many lights we have, you wouldn't believe me."

Georges Perrier

Those who have dined at Le Bec-Fin, one of the country's best *de luxe* French restaurants, know that Georges Perrier aims for perfection. They also know that he habitually hits the mark. The all-in-French menu is a tour de force, from the *bisque de homard* to *la charrette de desserts.* Between adjusting a *beurre blanc* sauce and double-checking the just-arrived Long Island foie gras, Georges also keeps a watch out for chips on the china, a bit of lint on a waiter's tuxedo, or one wilting tulip. His staff says he has "a thousand eyes," and remembers the year Georges had the entire restaurant repainted three times before he was happy with it.

That formidable attention to detail shaped Georges' home kitchen as well. In 1998, he bought a 25-year-old home in one of Philadelphia's upscale, "main line" communities. The spacious but ordinary (Georges says, "ugly") kitchen was naturally the first room to come under the chef's scrutiny. In preliminary discussions with his kitchen designer, Holly Mazzola, Georges laid out his sweeping concept: "I envision my new kitchen to be striking and contemporary, but it also must say 'Georges Perrier.' It must be a very, very practical kitchen, and I must feel good in it." He knew exactly which pieces of equipment he wanted, and why. He required plenty of counter space for staging courses or plating food, and enough room for six or eight people to work comfortably or to share a meal together in the kitchen.

Post-remodel, Georges' bright, sophisticated, hard-working kitchen is all that and more.

Working with New Jersey cabinet dealer Cornerstone, Georges first considered a top-of-the-line German manufacturer, but quickly discovered a local company, Heritage, whose work appealed to him. Georges had already decided that the cabinets should be white. He says with authority, "You never get tired of white. It doesn't go out of style, and it will always look good. I could have these for 20 or 30 years. And everything else you do will marry well with the white, too."

As a counterpoint to his white cabinets, Georges requested bold-colored, cheery, textured walls. Holly obliged by spackling the walls, sanding them down, then painting them with a yellow base and red-orange top coat that she toweled off for a vibrant effect. Serendipitously, the color was discovered inside a coffee cup Holly

A raised, Ultraglass counter tops Georges' stylish Brazilian granite

island. The cabinets in the "service" area store crystal and china.

A Franke sink with gooseneck faucet is used for washing delicate

glasses.

was using while meeting with Georges. He loves to tell the story of her exuberant "I've got it!" echoing through the house.

Georges likes beautiful tableware. He has amassed a remarkable array of grand china and antique crystal, which adds special luster to the formal dinner parties he loves to stage at home. His 18th- and 19th-century Baccarat and Saint-Louis pieces are protected in ripple-glass-front cabinets that line the kitchen's "service" area. After use, the delicate pieces are carefully washed by hand in the large Franke sink. Georges likes his gooseneck Franke faucet with "handles that are out of the way. You don't worry so much about cracking a plate or breaking a wine glass. When we do a party, we wash nothing in the dishwasher. It's not allowed."

The layout of Georges' 600-sq.-ft.-plus kitchen includes his "hot line," with a Viking six-burner cooktop, griddle, and flattop, two wall ovens—a gas Gaggenau and a Viking electric convection oven; a Viking bread warmer; and a custom-made Vent-a-Hood with two extra-quiet remote blowers. Each piece of equipment was carefully selected for its specific attribute. The Gaggenau oven draws Georges' special praise, "This, for me, is one of the best, without question. There are so many features. I can cook pizza on the stone. There's a rotisserie. It's a very sophisticated oven. I really love it, so I use it a lot." Likewise, the Viking oven: "It's extraordinary. There's a salamander inside—good for gratins. It's really a great, great oven. So precise."

At right angles to the range and ovens, the main sink area features double Franke basin, pull-out sprayer faucet, a hot- and cold-filtered water spigot, and an ASKO dishwasher, which Georges describes with Gallic enthusiasm as "very *silencieux*—no noise. It washes beautifully." The front of the dishwasher has a panel to match the cabinetry.

A Viking trash compactor and under-counter containers for recycling complete the arrangement.

For his ultra-modern center island—and for all the countertops—Georges selected a multicolor Brazilian granite. He recommends granite as a work surface because "you can set hot pots down on it wherever you want. Granite is so durable and I didn't feel that I needed a chopping block counter because I have plenty of small cutting boards that I move around." When he found the "Palladio" granite, Georges thought it looked like a work of art—like a Picasso.

Granite backsplashes flow around the kitchen, except behind the cooktop. There, Georges used a metallic-look ceramic tile, because he thought the granite might have seemed "too much, too heavy." The copper-finish tile from Questech is new on the market.

The angular, tri-level center island is crowned with a custom-made Ultraglass counter in the "Rain" pattern. The ¾-in.-thick, texturized, tempered glass usually takes eight months from order to delivery, but Georges had other plans. When the glass supplier was invited to Le Bec-Fin for dinner, the counters showed up in about three weeks. "I had to cry to get that counter," Georges says. It is supported by metal cylinders that extend through the glass and is cantilevered beyond the edge of the lower level. As soon as new bar stools arrive, Georges plans to use the stylish "breakfast bar" for his morning espresso.

Georges also planned the island's expanse for plating multi-course meals. "We're going to serve the food always from this island," he says. A Dacor plate warming drawer tucked into the island is convenient to the plating surfaces. The island also houses two Sub-Zero refrigeration drawers for vegetables and other ingredients used to garnish the table-ready plates.

So that he can really see the food and plates, Georges insists on an abundance of light in his kitchen. He says that "lighting may be the room's most important feature. If I told you how many lights we have, you wouldn't believe me." Holly confirms that there are more than 160 halogen light bulbs in the kitchen. Along with recessed ceiling lights, there are cabinet "flyover" lights above some of the cabinets and over the cooktop, under-cabinet lighting, and high-style FlosUSA fixtures over the island.

Opposite, "Flyover" lights are set in the shelving over the Viking six-burner cooktop. Two stacked ovens and a Viking bread warmer with humidifying action complete the cooking center. Copper-look ceramic tiles behind the cooktop have a fittingly warm yet high-tech style. *Below,* Tucked into the island, a Dacor warming drawer is handy for plating formal meals.

Opposite the island, Georges installed a Sub-Zero 700 series refrigerator with one large compartment and two separate drawers below. He uses the drawers for vegetables and fruit. Meat, cheese, and other dairy products are in the main refrigerator section. Georges likes to separate the two so delicate produce doesn't absorb odors.

Additional food storage is provided by a pair of oversize pantry cabinets. Although they look like the other cabinets from the outside, the pantries have pull-out metal racks, which Georges says are "the best way to store canned foods and glass jars. It's easy to see what you have on hand, and they're easy to clean. Nothing gets lost at the back of a shelf."

From the smallest detail to the overall concept, Georges thinks the design of his kitchen has worked out exceedingly well. He appreciates the kitchen's "flow," and thinks its contemporary plan suits his fast-paced lifestyle.

Georges started cooking in his native Lyon at about 12 years old. His grandmother and mother were big culinary influences. He calls his mother "a Renaissance woman," who speaks six languages, was a well-known doctor, and a "fabulous cook, a famous cook—for me." Although Georges' father wanted him to follow family tradition and become a jeweler or a doctor, Georges had staked out his cooking apprenticeship by the tender age of 14. He remembers his father said, "If he goes to work in a restaurant, he'll be back in a week." But once the determined young man began his new life, he never looked back. "That was it. I said, 'This is really the job of my life.'"

Under three-star mentors Jacques Picard, Michel Lorrain, and, especially, Guy Thivard at La Pyramide in Vienne, Georges' art developed quickly. At 23 he came to the states to work for Peter von Starck at La Panetière in Philadelphia. Just three years later, Georges eagerly launched Le Bec-Fin because, he says, it was time.

Almost 30 years later, Georges muses over newly unpacked mementos of Le Bec-Fin's early days as a tiny, nine-table restaurant. "It's wonderful when you move and you open up a box of things like the first menu you made. There was quiche Lorraine listed. 'You've

Left, Georges prepares to taste one of the wine selections for the evening's charity dinner. *Above,* Georges says the "Palladio" granite countertop reminds him of a Picasso.

got to be kidding,' I thought. Well, I came a long way, I guess. But that quiche was very, very good, I'm sure, even though it's not the kind of cooking I do now."

Le Bec-Fin's current offerings feature updated, light but intensely flavorful versions of classic French dishes. Duck consommé with truffle raviolis, scallop mousse with roasted pepper and *beurre blanc* sauces, and rack of lamb served on a bed of vegetables are examples. Georges uses much less cream in his creations today. "There are so many other things you can do to bring the flavors up. If I'm cooking fish, I want to taste the fish. You use too many ingredients or heavy sauces, it is ruined. It's much more difficult to keep a dish simple."

There's no doubt Georges has mastered that perfect simplicity. In 1993, *Esquire's* John Mariani wrote, "I would go to heaven without regret or resign myself to perdition if my last meal on earth included Perrier's sublime roast baby chicken with a sauce of pressed garlic cloves."

For a chef, it can also be difficult to juggle life's competing demands. "To be successful and to keep doing well, chefs have to

---

The French country table, made by a friend, occupies a cheerful breakfast corner. As a counterpoint to the glossy white cabinets, designer Holly Mazzola created textured, bold-colored walls.

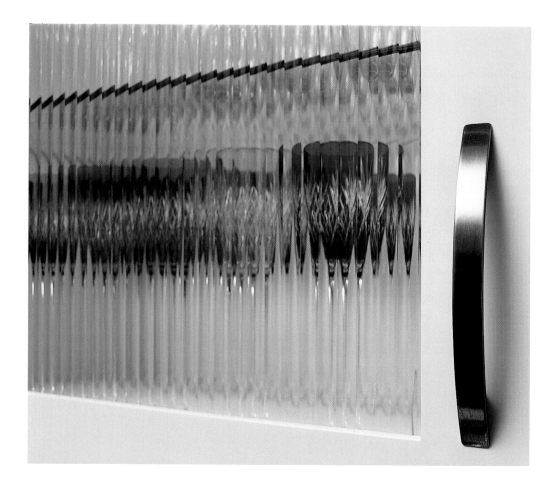

Right, Splashes of color show through the ripple-glass-front cabinets in the kitchen's "service" area, where Georges keeps his precious wine glasses. The sleek stainless-steel door handles are Italian. *Below,* Georges' knives are well organized, well cared for, and easy to access in a drawer.

make sacrifices. To balance everything is not easy because a restaurant is such a demanding profession—the hours, the work." In 1998, when Georges won the James Beard Foundation award for Best Chef in the Mid-Atlantic Region, he dedicated his award to his daughter, Genevieve, "for all the years when I was not home at night."

The whirlwind doesn't stop just because you've reached the top. "I've worked very hard to reach a certain level, and now I must do even more to stay there," he says. Somehow Georges' enthusiasm and other-worldly energy stay at their peak year after year. He added a bistro downstairs at Le Bec-Fin, opened Brasserie Perrier in January 1997, and put out *Georges Perrier: Le Bec-Fin Recipes* the same year.

That's not all. Future plans call for remodeling the rest of his home, writing another cookbook, and, possibly, opening a third restaurant, located somewhere besides Philadelphia. On this partic-

ular day, Georges turns his attention to a gala charity dinner to raise money for S.C.A.N., an anti-child abuse organization that is one of his favorite charities. "Tonight I'm giving a dinner for 18 people," he says. "It will raise $14,000. It's six courses with fabulous wines. I'll set up my dining room with flowers, beautiful china, silver, crystal—the best. I have chosen everything myself. It will be perfect!"

Lighting is very important in Georges Perrier's kitchen—there are more than 160 halogen bulbs in the room. The striking, modern fixtures now sparkling over the island were a real find; Georges spotted them in a magazine. Existing oak floors were refinished.

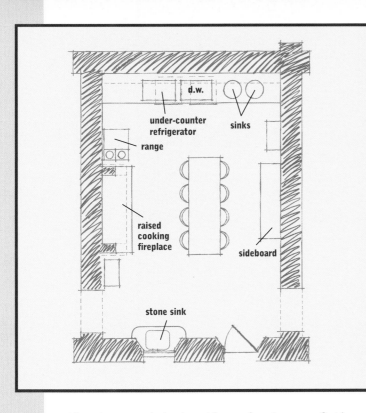

under-counter refrigerator

sinks

range

raised cooking fireplace

sideboard

stone sink

d.w.

"Everything that went into the design of the kitchen is local. I try to do the same thing when I am cooking, to use local things."

Chez Panisse

Although he has spent much of his career as chef at Chez Panisse, every summer Jean-Pierre Moullé returns to his house in Bordeaux, where he and wife, Denise Lurton, lead walking tours of the country-side, complete with stays at the Lurton family chateaux and dinners from the master's kitchen. Before coming to the United States, Jean-Pierre attended Ecole Hôtelier des Pyrénées and worked in European restaurants.

Opposite, *The centerpiece of Jean-Pierre's kitchen is its limestone fireplace.*

Jean-Pierre Moullé

For Jean-Pierre Moullé, there's home and then there's *home.* As head chef at Chez Panisse, the renowned California restaurant established by Alice Waters, Jean-Pierre spends much of the year in Berkeley, but every June, he and his family really go home, to France.

At the end of the school year, all the Moullés, including Jean-Pierre and Denise's two daughters, Maud and Elsa, and "Gypsy," the Labrador retriever, depart for Bordeaux to summer at their

The limestone walls create a warm atmosphere in the kitchen, which Jean-Pierre remodeled himself, using local materials and time-honored Bordelais methods of construction.

300-year-old farmhouse. There they relax, visit with friends and family, tend their vegetable garden, and make good use of their gracious country kitchen. As they have for the past 10 years, Denise and Jean-Pierre also lead a series of exclusive, week-long walking tours of Bordeaux's vineyards, stopping along the way to visit local cheese makers and markets. At night, Jean-Pierre cooks dinner for the group and teaches them about local dishes and ingredients. Denise, a member of one of Bordeaux's premiere wine-making families, adds her extensive wine knowledge to the evening. It could be called the perfect marriage of wine and food.

Jean-Pierre's interest in local flavor found another outlet while remodeling the family's ancient farmhouse. A long, L-shaped building, its thick, yellow limestone walls festooned with ivy, the house appears unchanged since the days when chickens scratched in the courtyard. Jean-Pierre designed the remodel and did the work largely by himself over 2½ years. He modified as little as possible in the kitchen—just enough to make it comfortable and functional.

The kitchen, a generously sized 14-ft. by 20-ft. space with stone walls and massive, exposed beams, was appealing but dark. Jean-Pierre recalls that the ceiling was completely black, indicating that the fireplace was not drafting properly. But what a magnificent fireplace it was. Though nearly 7 ft. wide and constructed of hefty lime-

*A neatly tiled counter with high backsplash extends across all 14 ft. of work surface, which features an inset pastry marble and cutting board, **left**. Knives are handy in a wooden rack over the food prep area. **Below,** Denise prepares the table for dinner; in French country homes, separate dining rooms are practically unknown. The limestone fireplace was raised up from the floor to create the hearth where Jean-Pierre does most of his cooking.*

stone blocks, it had graceful proportions and a warm, mellow color attesting to centuries of use. The fireplace was clearly the focus of the old room and is, just as plainly, the centerpiece of the Moullé kitchen today.

To bring the fireplace's cooking surface closer to the flue and, most important, to enable him to use it without having to bend over a floor-level fire, Jean-Pierre designed and built a new fireplace platform 2 ft. 8 in. high. Jean-Pierre discovered a local quarry that still cuts limestone like that of the original fireplace. Using precise measurements, stone workers cut the huge slab of stone that now forms the raised hearth. Underneath are storage areas for firewood and for grapevine cuttings, which are added to the cooking fire to give food extra flavor.

Also stored under the hearth is an array of specialized grills, "for salmon, for steak, for sardines—you name it," says Jean-Pierre. An elaborate, antique rotisserie was mounted in the fireplace to spit-roast meat. Jean-Pierre also uses copper pots and pans lined with stainless steel, cast-iron skillets, and pottery—made in nearby St. Émilion—which can be used over an open fire.

Beginning with the fireplace, function tempered with respect for the aged farmhouse guided the room's simple, practical design—the fireplace on one wall and the working surfaces, at a right angle, on the other. To avoid cutting into the thick stone walls of the room to install an exhaust system, Jean-Pierre positioned the La Cornue stove next to the fireplace. The draw from the fireplace serves the stove. A neatly tiled counter with a high backsplash extends across the 14-ft. work area, which features an inlaid pastry marble and cutting board as well as round, double sinks.

"Of course, since this is a French country house, you don't have modern things, like cabinets," quips Jean-Pierre. A collection of copper pots and pans hangs at-the-ready on the walls. Knives rest in a wooden rack over the cutting board. A simple strip of shelving displays pitchers, crockery, and more copperware. Oils and vinegars in graceful antique bottles rest on the counter. An antique sideboard, 6 ft. long, stores dishes and glassware.

The walk-in pantry provides storage for equipment that Jean-Pierre wants accessible but out of sight: an ice cream maker, food processors, and the main refrigerator. A small under-counter refrigerator stores drinks in the main part of the kitchen. Hanging fixtures illuminate work areas; the room also gathers light from oversized French doors the Moullés installed in the adjacent living room.

Large, hand-made, terra-cotta floor tiles match those laid centuries ago in other parts of the house. The worn, ancient tiles are beautiful in Jean-Pierre's eyes, as the new kitchen tiles will someday be.

Because they don't have a dining room, the Moullés instead have a large antique farm table that seats 12 comfortably. "Whether it's in Berkeley, or in France, we always eat in the kitchen. In the summer in Bordeaux we entertain a lot; it's nonstop with friends, family, and cooking students—everybody just loves to be in this kitchen."

Every morning Jean-Pierre—often with cooking students in tow—shops at the local markets to put together the meals for the day. The emphasis is always on what's in season. "I know the markets—what you're going to find, where and when," explains Jean-Pierre. "What

Denise and the girls pitch in to make sure there are plenty of home-grown vegetables and fruit for the entire summer. Jean-Pierre insists on cooking with fresh, seasonal foods.

Panisse kitchen, guiding the meal toward that state of perfection for which the restaurant is famous.

One of Jean-Pierre's most important tasks is to compose the daily menus for Chez Panisse. In consult with the kitchen staff, Jean-Pierre decides on seasonal meals such as sautéed scallop salad with summer chanterelles and leeks, and grilled squab with cabernet sauce. Other menus might feature roasted California sea bass with fennel and greens or grilled Willis Ranch pork with bay leaf and prune sauce.

Jean-Pierre grew up in France's northern provinces. Though he had no friends or relatives who were professional chefs, he explains that fine cooking "is in my family." His mother routinely cooked two meals a day for seven people. "That's a lot of practice. She cooked very well—and she still does," Jean-Pierre says. His earliest aspirations were to be a chef. He attended Ecole Hôtelier des Pyrénées in Toulouse for three years, then worked in restaurants in Europe before coming to the United States in 1976.

But his true introduction to the regional cooking of Bordeaux came in the kitchens of the Lurton chateaux. It was home cooking, not restaurant cooking—how to prepare Lamprey eels in red wine, for example, and the proper technique for pan searing a duck breast. The ingredients and dishes of Bordeaux are very different from those of Normandy. "My mother still pretends that she doesn't know what olive oil is," he laughs, since they use only butter and cream in the North.

All summer long the Moullés enjoy the ease, pleasure, and uniquely Bordelais quality of the old farmhouse kitchen. As Jean-Pierre puts it, "Everything that went into the design of the kitchen is local. I try to do the same thing when I am cooking, to use local things." Clearly, the authenticity of the kitchen is as important to Jean-Pierre as the authenticity of the regional foods he loves to prepare.

you eat in June is very different from what you eat in September. That's the way it's done here." He supplements market fare with vegetables from his garden. A neighbor supplies fresh eggs and chickens.

Come September, Jean-Pierre is back at Chez Panisse. In the morning, the cooking team goes over the dishes for that night's fixed-menu dinner. As the day progresses, Jean-Pierre oversees the selection and beginning preparation of the farm-fresh produce, local cheese, organically raised meats, and other specialty ingredients. By nightfall, the chef seems to be everywhere at once in the Chez

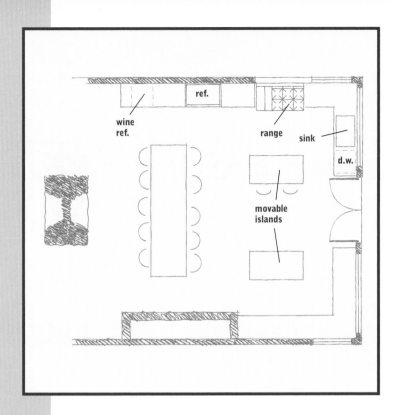

wine
ref.

ref.

range

sink

d.w.

movable
islands

"You know, this kitchen is about the size of
the entire apartment we had in New York."

**Bacchanalia
Floataway
Café**

Anne Quatrano and Clifford
Harrison are graduates of the
California Culinary Academy.
Bacchanalia, their restaurant, has
repeatedly been voted Atlanta's
Most Popular by Zagat's survey
and received Gourmet's 1997
Top Table award for Atlanta. Anne
and Clifford were on the Best
New Chefs list from Food & Wine
in 1996. Their second restaurant,
Floataway Café, opened in 1998.
Star Provisions market was
launched in 1999.

Opposite, "Everybody likes to
come out to the farm for dinner."

Anne Quatrano Clifford Harrison

When Anne Quatrano and Clifford Harrison drove down south from New York City for a spring-
time visit with old friends outside Atlanta, the life-long New Englander and the "hang-loose" guy
from Hawaii never imagined they'd find their true home.

Opposite, *Anne and Clifford's great room/kitchen is anchored by an impressive, split-face concrete block open fireplace. They planned to install a wood-burning oven, but ran out of money. The couple used such local build-ing materials as pine and recycled corrugated alu-minum roofing.* **Left,** *Clifford prefers to cook at home only on special occasions.* **Below,** *Vintage photographs show-case the farm's history.*

The couple had spent a few hard years working in Manhattan restaurants, living in a 500-sq.-ft. apartment on Amsterdam Avenue, and vainly trying to get their own restaurant off the ground. On their trip to Georgia they were entranced by the gently rolling countryside, huge old trees, and seas of blooming soybeans. Realizing they could live on a 60-acre farm that had been in Anne's mother's family for six generations, they were strongly tempted. After making the rounds of the best restaurants in Atlanta, they saw that there was room for their "Contemporary American" cuisine. Back in New York they took one look around their tiny apartment and decided instantly, "Hey, we're outta here." Within a month, they were Georgians.

Settling down in rural Bartow County, about an hour north of Atlanta, wasn't the easiest transition, however. The sultry Georgia summer was in full steam—literally—and the old house where Anne's mother lived as a child had long since crumbled. Anne and Clifford moved into a trailer on the property recently vacated by squatters. Over the next three years, the couple built a barn, culti-

vated the land, and concentrated on launching their restaurant, Bacchanalia, in the stylish Buckhead section of Atlanta.

Of necessity, they "lived, breathed, and ate" their restaurant, but they amassed ideas for their home, too. "We decided on a wraparound porch, because here we are on a farm," Anne says. The expansive kitchen was an obvious choice, with two professional cooks in the family. In addition, "We thought it should be open, with plenty of light," Clifford says. "A lot of what we wanted was the result of having lived in a double-wide trailer for three years," Anne observes.

The couple was committed to using building materials and a style that looked "right" in the landscape—including native pine and a steeply pitched roof of recycled, corrugated aluminum.

Anne designed the Summerland Farm house herself. "She did it all," Clifford says proudly. The house is configured in a T shape to maximize light, since a standard rectangle with deep wraparound porches makes for dark interiors, Anne says. She and Clifford preferred a barn-like look, with an interior open all the way up to the 22-ft. ceiling peak. The great room is anchored by an impressive, central fireplace in split-face concrete block.

An open, 24-ft. by 24-ft. space, the kitchen occupies half the great room. Anne planned a space that combines cooking and eating. "That idea is pretty foreign in a restaurant situation," Anne says, "but we wanted our home to be different from our work."

She selected a sturdy Wolf range with two different-size ovens and a griddle that she uses as a plate warmer. The Wolf "does everything we need it to do," Anne says. The range's broiler is a nice plus, but

Top, The six-burner Wolf range has two different-sized ovens—good for parties or dinner for two. Extra-deep cabinets made of local pine store large plates with ease. *Left,* Anne loves her "floating" tables for food preparation and plating meals. *Opposite,* The amount of space is Anne and Clifford's favorite feature of their new kitchen—it's as much as their entire apartment in Manhattan! Double doors lead to the old-fashioned covered porch. The floor is polished concrete, which is naturally mottled.

used only occasionally. Other major appliances include a side-by-side KitchenAid refrigerator/freezer, an under-counter wine cooler, and a Bosch dishwasher, which Clifford describes as hard-working and "silent." The pair would like to install a commercial dishwasher with a three-minute cycle, though, to handle their dinner parties. "We could ask two people over," Anne laughs, "but we always end up with 14, since that's how many chairs we have." Clifford explains, "Everybody likes to come out to the farm."

Clifford and Anne love their Blanco stainless-steel double sink, but regret not adding a second sink on the other side of the room's double doors. "It would have been great to have two sinks," Anne sighs.

The person who outfits Anne and Clifford's restaurants made the stainless-steel kitchen counters. The upper custom birch cabinets are 24 in. deep, instead of the standard 12 in., to house the chefs' oversized plates. Upper cabinets have glass doors because "I like to be able to see what's in there," Anne says. An old apothecary cabinet by the fireplace holds glassware. Anne and Clifford have more cabinets on order; "What happens in the restaurant business is that you collect tons and tons of china and glassware," explains Anne. In a number of under-counter spots, the couple installed deep, pull-out drawers. Anne says they're "very practical, because they hold more than shelves, and you can see what's in back."

Left, The couple's massive pine farm table was made locally by Hibberts Cabinet and Furniture. Anne says, "It feels good to have a big, strong table." For breakfast or the couple's dinners at home without guests, they often use one of the movable work tables. The tractor-seat stools were a farm-appropriate gift from Clifford to Anne. Dinner parties are usually for 14, "because that's how many chairs we have," Anne says. The stylish aluminum chairs are a 50-year-old Army design. **Above,** The 24-ft. by 24-ft. kitchen makes a great eat-in, live-in, entertain-in space.

Instead of a stationary island, Anne and Clifford invested in two commercial "floating" tables on large, lockable casters. "They work great," says Anne. "Every kitchen should have an island, but these are flexible as well." The tables came with under-counter storage racks for pots and pans. Anne added maple butcher block tops.

Dimmable "schoolhouse lights"—large globes hanging from the high ceiling—provide indirect lighting. Halogen fixtures under the cabinets supply task lighting.

The kitchen's warm-toned polished concrete floors are sealed, but, "I don't think you could tell if there was a stain on them; they're naturally mottled anyway," Anne says. "That's the glory of it." Radiant heat is built into the floors, but this extra warmth is rarely needed.

Windows high overhead open electronically, and warehouse fans "let the house breathe. They relieve some of the heat in the summer," Clifford explains. Ecologically minded and self-reliant, he would like to make better use of solar and wind power. He says, "My long-term goal is to be completely off the grid."

Although he seldom cooks at home, Clifford takes full charge of the couple's livestock and extensive vegetable garden. Aiming to

Anne looks around and says with a disbelieving shake of her head, "You know, this kitchen is about the size of the entire apartment we had in New York." She still seems amazed by the transformation in their professional and private lives.

"I cooked a lot as a young girl, because my mother didn't like to," Anne recalls. Anne's interest in cooking also was influenced by her grandmother, who was a great cook. "From the time I was 18, I've worked in restaurants," Anne says, "waitress, hostess, whatever." After college, she moved to Nantucket where, for seven years, she managed small restaurants and did some catering. The next step was cooking school, because to run your own restaurant—always her goal—"you really need to be educated on the kitchen side as well as the front of the house."

At the California Culinary Academy in San Francisco, Anne met Clifford, who says he "bailed her out in pastry class, because she didn't know how to make a butter cream." Clifford grew up in Hawaii. After a brief fling with academia—he wanted to be a history professor—he ended up in Sun Valley, Idaho, running a pizza place. Although he'd never had much exposure to cooking, Clifford found he loved it.

supply a majority of their restaurants' produce, Clifford has about four acres in herbs, fruits, and vegetables, including tomatoes, beans, corn, La Reine potatoes, melons, asparagus, and strawberries—all grown organically. Sharing the acreage with dogs, cats, and a flock of chickens are four Jersey dairy cows, a bull, and two horses. Anne says, "This year we'll have all four cows in milk, so we'll be experimenting with some cheeses we haven't made before—hard cheeses, Cheddar. We already do a lot with mozzarella, feta, fresh cheeses."

The couple's eat-in, live-in, entertain-in kitchen is dressed up with a big farm table, locally made of Georgia pine. "It feels good to have a big, strong table," Anne says. "Sometimes it's just the two of us eating at one end, and it still feels good." The aluminum chairs, a 50-year-old Army design, come from Emco in New York. For casual seating at one of the "floating" islands, Anne loves her tractor-seat bar stools—a Christmas gift from Clifford.

Above, An antique glass-front apothecary cabinet stores delicate glassware. The fireplace makes an open division between kitchen and living room. *Right,* A dinner party about to happen includes cauliflower soup, centerpieces of white flowers and cauliflower florets, one of Anne's 30 sets of dishes, and her grandmother's silver place settings.

When his pizza restaurant partnership broke up, he landed a job peeling potatoes at the Sun Valley Company's ski resort. Eighteen months later, he had moved up to jack-of-all-trades cook, rotating through the resort's more than 30 restaurants. Clifford enjoyed the work, but friends advised him that he needed to go to cooking school to advance his career.

After graduation from the C.C.A., Anne and Clifford moved to New York City. In the summer of 1992, they moved to Atlanta. Clifford says the hardest thing about the move was finding a location for their restaurant. Real estate agents "kept showing us little storefronts in strip malls and abandoned Del Taco buildings on busy corners." "Nobody had a clue as to our concept," a small, casual restaurant owned by the chefs and serving fine food at a reasonable price—no valet parking, no smoking, no hard liquor (just wine), and a *prix fixe* menu featuring fresh, organic ingredients.

One day, while cruising the Buckhead section of town, they saw "this old run-down house that had been an antique store. It had a sign on it that said 'Rent Me,' so we did," says Clifford. Bacchanalia opened in January of 1993, but "nobody knew who the heck we were.

Above, *The Francis Francis espresso maker is an eye-catching—and essential—part of the scene in the Quatrano-Harrison kitchen. Anne also loves her ice cream freezer, Acme juicer, Cuisinart, KitchenAid mixer, and cheese press; the couple makes cheese all summer long.* **Right,** *Jersey dairy cows graze on Anne and Clifford's Summerland Farm.*

Everybody was into a completely different scene," Clifford says. Following a three-month dry spell, "this famous chef came in, had a great meal, and told everybody about it. After that, we got busy."

Now, Bacchanalia is an upscale affair. "Because it was in a quaint little house, it seemed romantic and became a special-occasion restaurant," Anne says. "Guests expected certain things like premium ingredients and fine wines." Serving such specialties as ceviche of rockfish with shaved Oregon truffles, sweet butter-poached Maine lobster with asparagus and chervil, and pan-seared Georgia quail with sautéed apples, shiitake mushrooms, and cabbage, Bacchanalia has responded to the demand for an exceptional dining experience. Clifford says, "This is what a chef-owned restaurant should be. You can control everything—important when your name's on the door."

Having a hand in everything resulted in Bacchanalia's being named Atlanta's Most Popular restaurant by Zagat's survey for 1996, 1997, and 1998. Anne and Clifford were on *Food & Wine* magazine's list of Best New Chefs in 1995, and the restaurant was named *Gourmet*'s Top Table for Atlanta in 1997 and 1998. Not bad, for a pair of "talented youngsters...lighting up the fine dining scene like a couple of latter-day Shermans," as they were described in the *Atlanta Constitution.*

In 1998, the couple opened the Floataway Café, which, Clifford says, "harkens back to some of what we originally wanted to do with Bacchanalia." *The Atlanta Business Chronicle* dubbed the casual, warehouse restaurant "the elegant Buckhead restaurant's hip younger sister." Anne and Clifford upped the ante in 1999, launching a mid-town Atlanta market featuring fresh fish, meat, cheese, produce, wine, cooking classes, and, of course, a restaurant. Set in an old packing plant, the market overlooks downtown and is called Star Provisions. "We'd like to see people cook at home with the same quality ingredients we use in the restaurants," Clifford says.

At home, Anne and Clifford continue to expand Summerland Farm's output of vegetables, fruits, and dairy products, realizing that the more farm-fresh ingredients they provide for Bacchanalia and Floataway Café, the better the food will be. Local is always best. That message radiates from the large photograph hanging in Anne and Clifford's kitchen. It shows Anne's mother, about seven years old, playing with chickens in the same barnyard that's still right outside the door.

Anne designed the house herself. Wide, covered porches and aluminum roofs are squarely in the farmhouse tradition. Clifford takes charge of the garden and livestock. Four of their 60 acres are planted with herbs, tomatoes, beans, corn, potatoes, melon, and strawberries—all grown organically. The couple aims to supply vegetables and fruits for their own use and for Bacchanalia, Floataway Café, and Star Provisions.

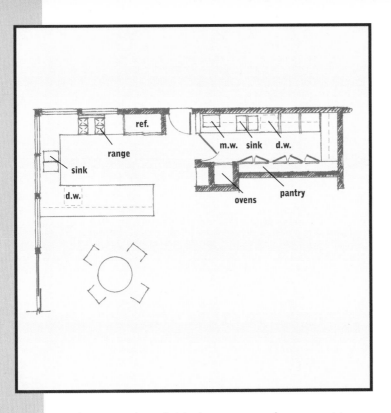

"Everything about the kitchen works pretty well, but then we had the opportunity to build it twice. That's rare."

Michael McCarty

California restaurateur Michael McCarty's over-the-top energy and enthusiasm influence everything he touches. Thanks to that relentless enthusiasm, Michael's—his legendary Santa Monica restaurant where "California Cuisine" was born—is still going strong after 20 years. It's also in character that when his cliffside home in Malibu burned down in the 1994 fire, Michael's response was to gear up, rebuild, organize his neighbors, and bounce back. Five years later, he says with a 100-watt grin, "Mudslides, fires, earthquakes, everything happens out here."

Perched 1,000 ft. up a steep hillside, overlooking an incomparable expanse of the blue Pacific and surrounded by vineyards, Kim and Michael McCarty's home is reborn. The McCartys bought the house in 1976 and remodeled a few years later, turning three rooms—dining room, kitchen, and den—into a spectacular, open living space loaded with glass doors and windows, wraparound decks, and, what is arguably, one of the best views in the world. Michael recalls, "We blew out the walls and put the dining and living areas across the front. The kitchen was at the back, but with a view out to the ocean." When they got the house just the way they wanted it, it burned down.

That traumatic event—Kim fleeing the flames in a station wagon with the kids and dogs, their home literally imploding in the 3,000-degree heat, and the loss of a big chunk of their priceless modern art collection—did not discourage them for long. Instead, it became an opportunity to start over. "We rebuilt the same house," Michael says. "We just tweaked everything to make it right the second time."

A result of that "tweaking" is a multi-kitchen arrangement that works well for the McCartys' lifestyle. Michael describes the three

spaces as "a daily use kitchen, a kitchen for the 'back of the house' stuff, and the kitchen on the big deck—very indoor-outdoor, very California." The main, or "daily use," kitchen is open to the great room and equipped to prepare family meals or to cook for guests. A second, separate cleanup area with pantry is housed behind doors in a back kitchen that's used for larger parties. The deck kitchen offers the ultimate in outdoor living with a wood-burning oven, a gas grill, and tables for 20.

Michael's is not open on Sundays, "so, we're open here," the host explains. Michael and Kim entertain by arranging tennis parties, wine tastings, gatherings around the pool, or alfresco meals. Frequently, the McCartys' parties benefit the arts; Kim is a painter and a member of the Board of Trustees of the Santa Monica Museum of Art. Michael's anniversary fund-raising event benefits that museum as well as other arts groups. When entertaining, Michael personally selects the produce from local farmers' markets. The wines come from the grapevines the guests can see all around them.

The McCartys' main kitchen, tucked into a corner of the great room, is fashioned from the same materials used throughout their

pizza?" almost constant. Michael laughs, "Whenever anybody mentions the fire, Kim says, 'Yes, now I have a *real* refrigerator.' "

A Thermador four-burner gas cooktop and Miele dishwasher round out the equipment in the main kitchen. Michael chose the cooktop because it was "the one with the most aesthetic appeal—the grill especially—and it works really well." He didn't want a hood intruding on the pristine space, so he installed a Viking down-draft system behind the cooktop. When not in use, it drops out of sight with the touch of a button. Michael occasionally supplements the vent's action by opening the window behind the cooktop.

A duplicate dishwasher and double sink are housed in the back kitchen. Kim and Michael like this arrangement because large-scale cleanup can go on during a party without disturbing guests. The back

home: vertical-grain Douglas fir for the ceiling and cabinetry, maple flooring, and plenty of glass. Vertical-grain Douglas fir is not normally used for cabinets because the wood is soft and because good, clear-grained fir is hard to find. "But we love it because it naturally turns this beautiful, warm color," Michael says.

The granite countertops are worth a closer look, too. Called "California Gold," the stone reveals bits of brown, cream, and softly shimmering gold that seem to float below the surface. "I love the little flecks of gold," Michael says. "I'm not normally a fan of granite because it tends to look unreal, but we finally found this." A deep edging piece runs around the perimeter of the counter, lending more heft to its appearance. The "eating side" of the counter is cantilevered to form a generous overhang, a perfect spot for Clancy and Chas to have a snack after school.

The new kitchen has the same layout as the pre-fire space, except that Michael "gave in" and installed a full-size Sub-Zero refrigerator. Previously, Kim had struggled with three under-counter refrigerators that Michael liked because they didn't block any light. The three-refrigerator system made such questions as, "Where's that leftover

kitchen also has two Thermador convection wall ovens, a Whirlpool microwave, and floor-to-ceiling pantry cabinets.

For the outside kitchen, Michael chose a Viking gas grill and an Italian, wood-burning pizza oven. The oven is available as a kit from Earthworks. As Michael says, "Because of where we are, with the

great weather and these views, we tend to grill outside all the time. And that wood-burning oven is just fabulous to fire up for parties."

Though just 21 when he moved to California, Michael was already as serious about the restaurant business as Kim was about her painting. He had grown up near New York City, in a family of four boys whose parents loved to throw big parties. "There was always lots of fabulous food, but they weren't into intellectualizing about it like people do today. It was more about the idea of getting together, the people, the conversation," Michael says.

The night before 15-year-old Michael left for a year of study in France, his parents took him to dinner at L'Aurent in Manhattan. He remembers clearly the mahogany-lined dining room, the food, and especially meeting the restaurant's owner, who electrified the room as he moved from table to table greeting his guests.

While in northern France, Michael lived with a local family. He describes them as "an aristocratic family that had lost their money, but still had style." That style included great meals—"Brittany is very food-oriented"—and more parties. The family also told Michael there were French schools that taught food and cooking. Never one to do things halfway, Michael enrolled in Ecole Hôtelier de Paris, the Cordon Bleu, and the Academie du Vin, graduating from all three. During his school years he also catered and opened a 22-seat restaurant in Paris. "That's where I first started the style of cooking I do," Michael says, "a mix of French and American."

On his return to the United States, Michael completed Cornell University's Summer Hotel Program. Later, he moved to Colorado and earned a degree in the business and art of gastronomy from the University of Colorado at Boulder.

Michael was attracted to California in the late 1970s when his parents moved to Malibu. His father had been named vice chancellor of Pepperdine University, and Michael came to visit from snowy Colorado. "It was January, but the weather here was in the 70s and the breeze was blowing off the ocean. I said, 'This is where I'm moving.'" He had already met Kim, who was attending art school in Boulder, so the two of them decided to try California.

As soon as Michael arrived, he became friends with chef Jean Bertranou of the famed Los Angeles restaurant L'Hermitage. Together

Opposite, *The view from Michael's "command center" stretches up the California coast and out to sea.* ***Above top,*** *The main kitchen is an integral part of the great room, finished with vertical-grain Douglas fir. The "outdoor kitchen"—a pizza oven and grill—are on the deck, beyond sliding glass doors.*
Above bottom, *Michael "gave in" to Kim and installed a full-size Sub-Zero refrigerator the second time they built the house. Before, they had three under-counter refrigerators, which didn't block light or views but made food storage difficult.*

they set up a duck farm north of Los Angeles, so that Bertranou could get local foie gras.

Michael's opened in 1979 in a vintage house near Santa Monica's beach. With its groundbreaking California cuisine, impressive wine cellar, contemporary art, secluded garden, and waiters in Polo shirts, "people from all over America would come to Michael's and think Los Angeles was the coolest place in the world," according to William Stadiem of *Buzz.* Michael recalls the 1980s as "10 solid years of insanity," a time when his restaurant was *the* place to dine and had became "an incubator for great chefs." Ken Frank, Jonathan Waxman, Mark Peel, Nancy Silverton, Gordon Naccarato, and Roy Yamaguchi all worked in Michael's kitchen. "We created a standard of how you run a restaurant," he says. "The food and wine were excellent, of course, but it looked beautiful, too."

Michael's continues to maintain its star quality. The once-startling California cuisine has become "classic" with such dishes as La Jolla striped bass with mango, Vidalia onions, and tarragon; shiitake and oyster mushroom pizza; and Montrachet goat cheese salad with roasted sweet peppers. A second Michael's, in Manhattan, opened in 1989, but while Michael splits his time evenly between the two establishments, the left coast is home.

Wherever he is, he has a story. Michael's 6,000 grapevines surrounding his home were planted because, "Every year, at the fire department's order, we'd spend thousands to have the bush cleared away," Michael explains. "We were having this wild party and Dick Graff—who owned Chalone and Acacia wineries—was here and I'd just gotten the bill for the brush clearing. I said, 'That does it,' and asked him to help me plant grapes instead. Every square inch that wasn't built on was going to have vines that they couldn't ask me to remove." Michael's first wine was bottled in 1989. Five vintages later, the vineyard didn't prevent the fire, but the dormant vines survived to produce again.

As for his newly rebuilt kitchen, Michael would change nothing. "Everything works pretty well, but then we had the opportunity to build it twice. That's rare." He likes best "the idea that it's a major part of our living space, but it blends right in." He adds, looking out to miles of ocean, "this isn't a bad command center right here."

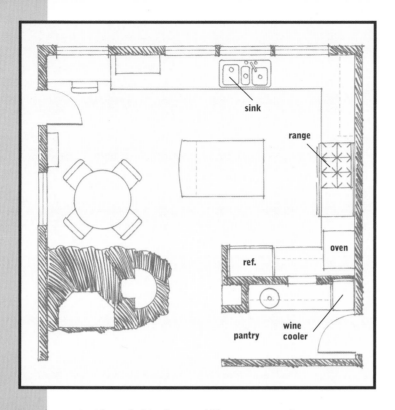

Frank McClelland's award-winning restaurant, L'Espalier, is Boston's premier spot for elegant, special occasions. Frank's career took off at the acclaimed Harvest Restaurant in Cambridge, Massachusetts, but he first learned about growing and preparing top-quality ingredients on his grandparents' New Hampshire farm. He calls his cuisine "classical, New England, whimsical, based on a concentration of flavor and stripped down to simplicity."

Opposite, Frank uses his wood-burning oven daily to cook a whole meal or just a loaf of bread.

"I blocked out the kitchen like a series of dance steps, actually working out the actions."

Frank McClelland

Frank McClelland spent much of his childhood on his grandparents' New Hampshire farm, where he learned cooking and gardening and where his New England roots began to grow deep. So it wasn't surprising that life in a third-floor flat over his upscale Back Bay Boston restaurant grew a bit confining.

"Catherine and I lived above L'Espalier for nine years before we moved out to the country. When we had our third child and got a big dog we just couldn't live in the city anymore," he says. Besides, Frank wanted more room for vegetable gardening than his tiny rooftop plot allowed.

In 1996, the couple looked for a house well outside Boston but within easy commuting distance for the chef, who insists on being in his restaurant's kitchen six nights a week (and who was accustomed to simply walking down the stairs to work). Initially, Frank and Catherine wanted an old house with a strong sense of history. When they couldn't find an existing property that appealed to them, they decided to build. Their site was a rolling, wooded piece of land with gentle views of a nearby pond and lots of level, sunny ground for serious vegatable gardening.

Presented with the luxury of a completely blank slate, Frank and Catherine began to consider the house's overall orientation and placement of rooms. Their land is surrounded by a state park on three sides, so they wanted to take advantage of the fact that nothing would

*Opposite top, Frank puts the handsome oak and granite island to work. He appreciates his new kitchen most for its layout, which makes for a seamless flow of work. Frank's Wolf range and Northland refrigerator are close at hand when he works at the island. **Opposite bottom,** Frank installed a tall faucet above the versatile six-burner range. **Left,** He makes good use of high cabinets for storing less-used equipment, which he reaches with a custom-made ladder.*

Aside from privacy and good access to the outdoors, Frank wanted natural light, high-performance but easy-to-use equipment, and a comfortable (but not rustic) country feel to the kitchen. The large but cozy 14-ft. by 20-ft. space was set in a back corner of the house and opens onto an old-fashioned covered porch and patio. To maximize sunlight, architect Larry Frej proposed an impressive bank of small-paned windows stretching across one entire wall and soaring up to the extra-high ceiling. The result is a graceful blend of historic and modern styles that provides all the light their hearts desire.

Although the windows are a distinct and carefully planned benefit, they precipitated other design considerations. "I wanted a country kitchen—no flash," says Frank, so after the brown-gray granite counters were polished, they were honed to take off the shine. "We have so many windows, and this is a very bright kitchen. We often have 10 hours of sunlight here, so we had to do something about the glare" from the countertops. Nighttime lighting consists of suspended lamps specially designed by Phillipe Starck and strategically placed task lighting. "Lighting is very, very tricky," Frank admits.

Directly beneath those spectacular windows, Frank positioned the Elkay sink and Bosch dishwasher. Flip-out, plastic-lined drawers below the sink provide mess-free storage for sponges and vegetable scrubbers. A Franke faucet pulls out to become a hand-held sprayer. Large trash containers hide below the sink.

In keeping with the country ambiance, the McClellands installed oak floors and mellow, white oak cabinets built to look like antique furniture. The granite-topped island on carved legs is especially evocative of a bygone era, and as soon as the McClellands find the

be built on the adjacent land in the foreseeable future. "We have parks all around us, so it will pretty much stay like this," he says. They decided to create a private side of the house, away from the street and looking through the trees to the pond. Both thought it made sense to settle the all-important kitchen in the heart of that space, surrounded by a family room, dining room, and butler's pantry.

Opposite, Keppler, Annie, and James are right at home in the kitchen. A graceful bank of windows pulls in natural light and draws the eyes to the outdoors. The hanging lights are a Philippe Starck design. Because of glare from the granite counters, the McClellands honed the granite to a more countrified and easy-on-the-eye matte finish. **Left,** The butler's pantry leads from the kitchen to the dining room. A good place for storing formal glassware and serving pieces, the pantry also houses an 80-bottle Northland wine cooler. The pass-through helps dispatch food from range to dining room.

perfect stools, the island will have seating at the rounded end. At the other end, a rack custom-designed for Frank's oversized spice bottles is concealed in the island, yet easily accessible from the range.

Cooking options are extensive in this kitchen. Frank decided on a six-burner, two-oven Wolf range "because so many people rave about them, and they're very easy to keep clean and to operate at home." He also wanted a domestic range that Catherine could work with and, "she has become very proficient using the Wolf." A handy water source above the burners makes preparing large pots of pasta a breeze—even for the petite Catherine. All in all, "The big range is really used. We cook at home every night because we believe in giving our family the most nutritious and balanced meal we can." Besides, the griddle works beautifully for those buttermilk pancakes Frank loves to make for children Keppler, Annie, and James. (As befitting the children of a famous chef, other favorite meals include fish, roast lamb, and polenta with duck confit and chopped herbs.)

To supplement the range, Frank chose a Blodgett convection oven for letter-perfect baking. He rounded out the business end of the kitchen with stock stainless-steel commercial kitchen counters, roll-

out shelving for pots and pans, and a Northland refrigerator. Frank's only regret is that he should have bought a Northland with two refrigerator compartments and a very small freezer, rather than the large side by side. "The idea was to build a professional 'shop' area in one corner but to integrate it with the rest of the kitchen, which would be very homelike," says Frank. Also in the "shop" area, a convenient pass-through to the butler's pantry works well for getting formal meals or hot hors d'oeuvres out to the dining room.

The Northland wine cooler in the butler's pantry holds 80 bottles and is also used for bottled water and soda. Frank appreciates the fact that the cooler is built like an industrial unit and the compressor can be pulled out for servicing. "It'll last 30 years or more." The pantry contains storage for glasses and table linens as well as a round copper sink and Herbeau faucet.

Near the pantry door, the McClellands installed an oven for open-fire cooking. The kitchen side of a massive fieldstone chimney boasts a Renato wood-burning oven, while a fireplace opens to the family room. Built according to time-honored Italian-stone masonry techniques by Peter Giordano, the chimney has a fabulous natural

draw—"a result of good design and superior craftsmanship," says Frank. The oven, with its modern firebrick interior, can get up to 800°F. "You make the fire in front and then push it to the back," Frank advises. "I've done a multitude of different things with it," he says. "You can cook your whole meal in the oven or a loaf of fantastic bread. I've even cooked smoky oysters right over the fire, and every-

body wants me to roast a turkey or make a tagine," or Middle Eastern stew. Giordano also built the large fieldstone fireplace outdoors on the McClellands' patio.

Other custom features in the kitchen include a handsome wooden ladder, built to access high cabinets where Frank stores large, less-often-used equipment, and a utensil rack to the left of the range. The McClellands' centuries-old dish collection is displayed in a glass-front cabinet built to look like heirloom furniture.

But it's not equipment, furniture, or specific features Frank cites when asked what he likes best about his new kitchen. "What I appreciate most is the way the kitchen functions. How easy it is. The movement and flow. You come up from the garage with your dry goods and produce, you can just drop your bags on the island, and then put everything away—the fridge and food storage cabinets are right here," he explains. He also likes the fact that the kitchen works just as well for a small crowd of cooks working together as it does for the lone cook.

"I feel that movement is critical when you're laying out a kitchen," Frank explains. "I blocked it out like a series of dance steps, actually working out the actions needed to make a particular dish. Facing the stove, then turning 180 degrees to the right to get spices and chopped onions on the island, then reaching the other way to get a ladle, stepping to the refrigerator for butter while grabbing a pan from the cabinet here." In kitchen design Frank believes, "the layout is number one, your equipment is number two, and aesthetics are last."

Just as carefully, Frank laid out his extensive vegetable and herb gardens. He is serious about the gardening techniques his grandfather taught him, and he wants to instill that same love of gardening in the next generation. "I put brick paths everywhere so the kids can help in the garden. And I make a fun game out of the weeding."

When Frank says, "I don't know if I like gardening or cooking better," it rings true. "My main influence was that I had the good fortune of growing up and spending a lot of time with my grandparents, who were retired and lived on a farm in New Hampshire. That's where I learned to garden and cook. At the turn of the century, my grandfather's mother was a chef with her own catering company in Europe. His grandmother grew up in New York City and was taught to cook by

Left, For cooking outdoors, the McClellands use their fieldstone and brick fireplace. Complete with motorized rotisserie and blue-stone counters, the barbecue area works for a crowd or for just a boy and his dog. **Above,** Frank loves vegetable gardening. He laid brick paths throughout the garden so the kids could help.

her mother-in-law, so she was a wonderful cook, too. I got great inspiration from my grandmother." It didn't hurt young Frank's culinary education that his grandparents were friends with many of the European chefs who came to New England to open inns.

Later, Frank worked in kitchens during summer vacations and eventually followed Andre Mayer to the acclaimed Harvest Restaurant in Cambridge, Massachusetts. By 1984, Frank was working at the Country Inn in Princeton, Massachusetts, where he was named one of the country's top 25 chefs by *Food & Wine* magazine. Frank and Catherine bought L'Espalier in 1988 because, as he says, "I wanted the freedom of my own kitchen."

L'Espalier, housed in a refined 1886 Back Bay mansion, has evolved into Boston's premier spot for elegant, romantic dinners. The luxurious, special-occasion restaurant garnered four stars from *The Boston Globe* and the *Mobil Travel Guide,* thanks to such exquisite dishes as pan-roasted Vermont baby pheasant with chanterelles, foie gras croutons, and Pinot Noir huckleberry sauce, or grilled lobster and risotto with fava beans. And as a true sign of its popularity with diners as well as with critics, L'Espalier consistently receives top ratings from Zagat's survey.

You could say that Frank and Catherine McClelland are admirably settled. L'Espalier is at its peak; their country kitchen is beautifully finished; and they have a perfect place for the family—and the vegetables—to put down their own New England roots.

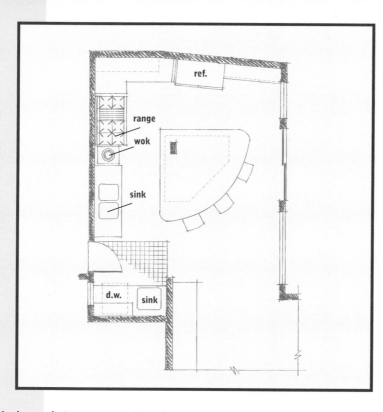

"The island is a really big piece and I didn't want to fix it somewhere and then be stuck with it. You never know exactly what you want when you haven't lived in a space."

**Dahlia Lounge
Etta's Seafood**

When Tom Douglas landed in Seattle at age 19, he quickly turned an avocation for cooking into a successful career. His first restaurant, Dahlia Lounge, has been a critically acclaimed trend-setter since it opened in 1989. Etta's Seafood followed in 1995. Tom's most recent entry to the Seattle restaurant scene is Palace Kitchen. All Tom's restaurants showcase his daring Northwest, Asian-influenced cuisine. He was the 1994 winner of the James Beard Award for Best Chef of the Pacific Northwest.

Opposite, *Tom loves his restaurant-style double sinks with cutting board top.*

Tom Douglas

Tom Douglas refers to himself as a "big dude." And once you see his home kitchen, you understand that the sobriquet fits. His kitchen is a big daddy, too. The large, hard-working room, with its massive center island, oversize wok, six-burner range, and double commercial prep sinks, gives Tom the equipment and elbow room to cook comfortably at home.

Tom's interest in easy-access kitchen storage led him to design this updated "spice rack," *left.* Magnetic strips attached to the refrigerator cabinet hold small metal boxes. ***Opposite,*** The cherry wood center island is massive but mobile, thanks to heavy-duty casters. The top is a maple chopping block, so there's always room for preparing food, even on a large scale. The metal bar chairs with sumptuous velvet cushions are Italian.

The owner of three highly successful Seattle restaurants—Dahlia Lounge, the Palace Kitchen, and Etta's Seafood—also wanted a suitable place to cook on a grand scale; he frequently uses his home kitchen for charity dinners, cooking classes donated to worthy causes, and staff parties for his 200-plus employees. You could say that Tom's heart matches the rest of him.

Though Tom landed in Seattle at age 19 with no formal food training, he always worked in restaurants, first as employee and later as owner. That experience, combined with a serious amount of eating at the best restaurants ("I spent as much on food as I would have in college tuition") served him well. He opened Dahlia Lounge in 1989 because he had quit one job "naively thinking someone would offer

me another one right away…but didn't." With a $50,000 loan from an uncle, Tom and his wife, Jackie, started their own restaurant. "We were expecting a baby—we needed a paycheck," says Tom. Ten years and three restaurants later, Dahlia's success as a mecca for Northwest, Asian-influenced fusion food has made all else possible, including the Douglas's newly remodeled home overlooking Puget Sound.

Tom and Jackie with their 8-year-old daughter, Loretta, bought a plain vanilla 1950s ranch house three years ago. Tom is quick to point out that this was not their dream home—"we like houses with molding and details"—but its panoramic view was too good to pass up. They bought the house and immediately began a major remodel

that eventually left very little of the house unchanged. While the family lived downstairs in a basement apartment, the work went on over-head. Tom recalls, "We just started going for it. Right away we took it down to the studs."

With the upstairs gutted, the Douglases suddenly realized that they needed to make some important planning decisions about how to build out the space. Tom and Jackie knew all along that the former family room would be an ideal location for the new kitchen; it was a large, 15-ft. by 16-ft. space, had easy access to the garage for bring-ing in groceries, was open to the future dining room, and connected to a deck so they could eat while enjoying the spectacular view. Tom did a lot of the heavy work himself, including the demolition and

installing insulation and drywall, and got help from a local contractor with the jobs that required more skill.

Because the outside wall of the house was built at an angle, the kitchen is laid out on two sides of a triangle. One wall holds the prep sinks, wok, and range, while the other has a baking area and a Sub-Zero refrigerator. An extra-large, movable island built of cherry with a maple butcher block top has deep drawers for food storage and a built-in garbage bin. The baseball-diamond-shaped island is on heavy-duty wheels so it can be shifted for cleaning or moved out of the way when a crowd is expected. It can also fit snugly against the wall in one corner, increasing floor space and providing an ample buffet for large platters of food. Tom explains, "The island is a really big piece and I didn't want to fix it somewhere and then be stuck with it. You never know exactly what you want when you haven't lived in a space."

Tom wanted commercial elements in his kitchen for practicality and because they work so well. He designed a cutting board that fits over one side of the double sinks, so "when I'm prepping racks of ribs for the barbecue, I have water right there and I can clean up easily without getting grease all over the island." A large pot rack and magnetic strips for knives and other tools are mounted over the prep sinks so that Tom's equipment is out and available. He also made good use of "stock" commercial stainless-steel sinks, rolling units with hotel pans, and shelving from a restaurant-supply store, integrating them artfully into the overall design. Tom says that these prefabricated units are "really pretty cheap," so he installed them where he could and then filled in with more expensive custom-made equipment, counters, and cabinets.

Because Tom wants his equipment and ingredients handy, his is not a cabinet-intensive kitchen. He is proud of his special spice rack that is made up of board-mounted magnetic strips that hold small stainless-steel tins. Spices and ingredients that can be bought in metal containers—baking powder, crab boil, or paprika, for instance—go on the rack immediately, while others need only be transferred to the appropriate tin.

The former powder room on one side of the kitchen was turned into a small but efficient cleanup alcove. Although open to the kitchen,

Opposite top, *The oversize Imperial wok is an integral part of Tom's "hot line" and is necessary equipment for preparing his signature Northwest-Asian dishes.*
Opposite bottom, *Tom appreciates his speedy commercial Hobart dishwasher after big parties. The hand-held sprayer quickly rinses a rack of dishes. Colorful Pratt & Larsen floor tiles are easy to clean. Quilted stainless forms a stylized backsplash.* **Left,** *A pot rack and wall-mounted magnetic strips ensure that Tom's most frequently used equipment is always close at hand.*

the alcove is shielded from view from the dining room so guests don't see dirty dishes while lingering after dinner. The commercial Hobart dishwasher, extra-deep sink, and pull-down spray hose streamline cleanup jobs. "I got so sick of getting up in the morning after a big party and having 12 loads of dirty dishes to do," says Tom. The Hobart's 90-second cycle makes washing up a breeze. A ceramic tile floor in the alcove is easier to maintain than the oak floors in the rest of the kitchen. Again with an eye for a bargain, the Douglases chose top-of-the-line Pratt & Larsen tile, but found factory seconds. Tom wishes he had continued the tile floor along the entire "hot line," and may make that change in the future.

The stainless-steel backsplashes are a challenge to keep clean because they spot easily. But Tom and Jackie fell hard for the look of the "quilted" design and thought it added a nice touch to the '50s-style house. Routine cleaning includes a rubdown with stainless-steel polish and a final coating of baby oil for a satiny gleam.

Tom designed the sideboard, **above,** *which stores—and shows off—china, stemware, and platters. Red and ivory marble tops the buffet and sideboard.* **Left,** *Garbage collection is built into the island, as are copious drawers for boxes, bags, and other large packages of dry foods.*

For his range, Tom settled on a DCS domestic model with six burners, a griddle, and two ovens, one with a convection option. Tom decided on the domestic unit because they are better insulated. Domestic ranges also don't heat up the kitchen as much and stay warm for a long time after they're turned off. The opposite is true of commercial ranges, which are designed to heat up and cool off very quickly.

Tom uses his large, freestanding, Imperial wok frequently. "It's great to have. If you're trying to do a whole course for a lot of people in one of those little woks on the stove, it's just ridiculous." The wok runs at a staggering 120,000 BTUs and "sounds like a rocket ship when I turn it on," says Tom. He likes the wok for lobster, shrimp, and shiitaki potstickers or fried Dungeness crab with lemongrass and ginger, a popular dish at Etta's Seafood.

Shellfish has long been a favorite of Tom's. Growing up in Newark, Delaware, Tom and his seven brothers and sisters loved to go crabbing. "We'd just go down to the bridge, drop a chicken neck down on a line, and there you are, blue crab for dinner," he remembers. When he began researching local Seattle menus, Tom was amazed to find that no restaurants featured crab cakes, even though the local crab is spectacular. "Go figure," he thought, and immediately offered them as a specialty. They've been his restaurants' mainstay ever since.

The Douglases designed all their restaurants themselves. Other instances of cross-pollination between home and restaurant are evident in the dining room. Creamy red and ivory marble on the buffet and sideboard were cut from a larger piece used in Dahlia Lounge. The sideboard houses stacks of tableware from all three restaurants. It also was cleverly designed with racks that simultaneously store and display a collection of large, colorful platters. Cheerful red and yellow walls echo in brighter hues at Dahlia.

The dining room table was also a family project. Tom, Jackie, and Jackie's father crafted it from East African bubinga. Tom says he wanted the look of a solid picnic table made of a beautiful wood. The four slabs of bubinga, 14 ft. long and 4 in. thick, were trimmed down to the final 10-ft. length. Leftover pieces became the table legs. Because the table was built "on its back," Tom wasn't sure it would be level when it was turned over. And, because it weighs 1,000 pounds, "we were only going to turn it over once," he says. There was a tense moment when the table was eased onto its legs. But like most of Tom's ventures, it worked out just fine.

Dahlia Lounge has been a critically acclaimed trendsetter since it opened in 1989, with offerings such as house-smoked salmon hash with Yukon gold potatoes, fried quail eggs and white truffle oil, or venison on celery root gratin with cranberries. Etta's Seafood followed in 1995, serving a dazzling array of fresh seafood as well as familiar comfort food. In a 1997 review of the newly opened Palace Kitchen, *The New York Times* characterized Tom as someone "who had already earned a reputation for daring, savory cuisine," and the local press styled the restaurant "the place to be."

At home, the kitchen is the place to be for all the Douglases. For big parties, Jackie enjoys lending a hand as Tom's prep cook. "My personal Veg-o-Matic," Tom says with a grin. The kitchen's space and flexibility are Tom's favorite features. "It flows like a kitchen should flow. When you walk in, there's a spot to put your groceries down. I can chop right where I want to. Everything's where I want it—or I can move it where I want it." Tom's kitchen is like his restaurant concepts—big, innovative, and successful.

Tom's parents enjoy a glass of wine and the spectacular view of Puget Sound. Tom, Jackie, and Jackie's father built the dining room table of dense African bubinga. Ruby, the Douglases' Brittany spaniel, waits patiently for Loretta and Jackie to return from a fishing trip.

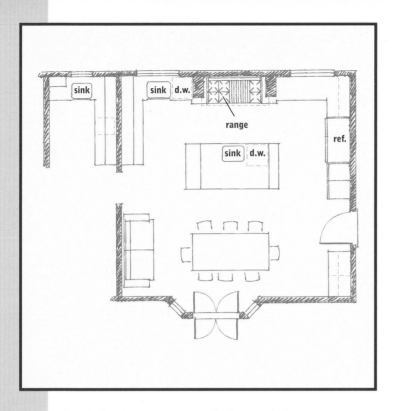

"When we decided to remodel and improve our kitchen space, we made it as nice as possible because we want to spend a lot of time in there as a family."

Terrance Brennan

Terrance Brennan has come a long way from his days of burning rubber in the parking lot of his parents' sandwich and pizza place in suburban Virginia. Now he's chef and proprietor of Picholine—an elegant, critically acclaimed restaurant serving French Mediterranean fare on Manhattan's Upper West Side—husband, father of three (Ryan, Caroline, and Carson), and new homeowner. He can look back on those boyhood antics in a beat-up Opel Cadet and smile.

Picholine

Owning one of Manhattan's most sophisticated and successful restaurants is a dream fulfilled for Terrance Brennan. After stints at hotels in Washington, D.C., a job at Le Cirque in New York, and apprenticeships at three-star restaurants in Europe, he opened Picholine as a casual neighborhood bistro. Soon the perfectionist chef transformed Picholine into a fine-dining establishment serving innovative, French Mediterranean-inspired dishes.

Opposite, *Working at their stepped-down counter, Caroline and Ryan let dad help roll out the cookies.*

The spacious, light-filled country kitchen features custom-made cabinets and Viking appliances. The range area is "the heart of the kitchen," and its well-crafted cabinetry reflects that theme. Other cabinets have an antique look, such as the open-shelf cabinet with arched top. The range's six burners, griddle, grill, and two ovens give the chef plenty of cooking options. All appliances are the same brand because Terrance appreciates their clean lines and high quality.

In late 1997, Terrance and his wife, Julie, bought their 100-year-old white clapboard house in New York's Westchester County. They knew it would be a mountain of work to turn the neglected property into their dream home, but after cramped city quarters with two young children and a baby on the way, the rambling house on several acres held strong appeal. The Brennans moved into their new home on New Year's Eve. "I couldn't believe it, looking around," Terrance recalls. "It was a mess, a total wreck, so Julie and I called our babysitter, dressed, and went out to a party." Next year would be soon enough to begin planning their remodel.

Left, *Equipment hangs over the center island from a custom pot rack accented by internal lighting that floods work surfaces below. A bank of drawers, **below,** makes the island more than just a place for cutting and washing vegetables. Some extra-deep drawers are made of baskets.*

The kitchen was their first target. The couple made wish lists—high-end appliances, enough space for a dining table and comfy sofa (so the entire family could "hang out" in the kitchen), and cabinetry that reflected the house's English country ambiance. Then Julie methodically researched ideas in magazines, design books, and vendors' showrooms. After 20 years of working in professional kitchens, Terrance knew what was important to him—plenty of uncluttered counter space, a powerful range with lots of options, separate food preparation and cleanup areas, and convenient storage.

The Brennans' ideal kitchen was a far cry from the one they moved into. Terrance recalls that the old kitchen was "horrible": small and dark, with little counter space, an awkward array of cabinets stuck in the center of the room, and an inconvenient refrigerator alcove. None of the major components could be salvaged; the old 1920s stove wouldn't even light.

The couple decided to create one large room by merging the kitchen with the tiny back porch, laundry, and bathroom. They began by opening the 19-ft. by 21-ft. room to the sunny flagstone terrace via

French doors. Next, they decided to split the kitchen down the middle, with "working" and "relaxing" areas divided by a large central island. The range, sinks, food preparation areas, and refrigerator comprise the working side; a dining table and sofa create a relaxed living space opposite.

For cabinets, Terrance and Julie knew they wanted a country look that would be compatible with their home. Although they considered many options, they quickly settled on cabinets from Christian's, a high-end, custom English cabinetmaker.

The basic design centered around the range area, because it was conceptually "the heart of the kitchen," says Terrance. Woodwork above the range suggests a fireplace mantel and does double duty by minimizing the vent hood and providing a display shelf for favorite pieces of china. In the middle of the room is a 4-ft. by 10-ft. island with overhead pot rack. Sealed limestone countertops form a handsome, hard-working surface. Terrance says, "I wanted a lot of counter space so we could have three or four friends or family members working at once." One section of counter was made lower than the rest: "If the kids want to join in, they can have fun mixing up something there." The ample island also houses a prep sink and dishwasher, plus extra storage for equipment, dry foods, and such everyday family essentials as crayons.

A cleanup sink and second dishwasher occupy a prime position to one side of the stove beneath large casement windows. Julie chose

Picholine is known for its marvelous cheese course, dispensed with flair by maître fromager Max McCalman, who offers 50 different cheeses. At home, Terrance enjoys composing a smaller, but nicely ripened, selection of cheeses for guests. A food prep sink in the island makes quick work of washing fruit. A cleanup sink is stationed under generously sized casement windows and beside the dishwasher to the left of Terrance's big range.

a big Kohler apron sink for the cleanup area because she likes the "farmhouse" touch it adds. The Brennans specified additional counter space to the left of the cleanup sink, plus cabinets with beveled glass fronts for dish storage. The antique feel results from the design of the cabinets and from the distressed look added with a tiny paintbrush by artist Nancy Kirk. To the right of the range is another stretch of work surface, an open-shelf display cabinet with vintage-style arched top, the food pantry, and Viking refrigerator.

Terrance bought all the appliances from one manufacturer to ensure design consistency. He chose Viking because he finds the look of Viking products clean and sophisticated and because the appliances are high quality. "I love the big stove," says Terrance. "The burner configuration has turned out well—four and two, separated with a griddle and grill. We started out using the griddle just for

A Viking bread-warming drawer is stationed between the kitchen and butler's pantry and formal dining room. Terrance appreciates the warmer because he used to put bread in the oven and forget about it. Now the bread is perfectly warmed and never burned.

pancakes for the kids, but now we're using it for everything. It's great for mock stir-fry." The hood functions so efficiently that "I can even grill steaks inside." Both of the range's two ovens convert to convection mode with the flip of a switch.

Other professional Viking equipment in the Brennans' kitchen includes two dishwashers ("but we could have used three; we should

The compact, efficient butler's pantry houses glassware and cups as well as a Viking under-counter ice maker and Kohler apron sink. There's plenty of counter space for washing delicate stemware, pouring coffee, or serving desserts. The space works well, though Terrance wishes he had installed a third dishwasher there, which he may add in the future.

Left, A kitchen door leads to an inviting, old-fashioned porch and a swimming pool beyond. Next to the door and behind a comfortable family dining table, Terrance positioned two Viking wine coolers—one for red wines and the second for white wines, bottled water, and soft drinks. *Below,* In the backyard, French doors open to a flagstone terrace, where the Brennans enjoy cooking on their gas grill and where the younger set entertains friends.

have put another one in the pantry"), bread warmer, ice maker, garbage disposal, and two undercounter wine coolers—"one at red wine temperature and the other colder, for white wine, water, and sodas." A Viking gas-fired grill is just beyond the French doors on the terrace.

When it came time to decorate, Terrance ceded control to Julie. She chose a large dining table, a cozy sofa, and hand-made Anne Sacks accent tile hand-painted with colorful fruit to match the sofa. Julie plans to add a green and black diamond pattern to the oak floor to give it "a softer, more countrified feel." Low-voltage under-cabinet lights subtly illuminate the countertops and highlight the limestone's natural patterns.

Now that most of the work is finished, Terrance has just a few regrets. He originally wanted a built-in, concealed garbage can, and

he would have liked more large drawers for pots and pans. Overall, though, the kitchen is just about perfect for the Brennan family. The layout and the spaciousness of the kitchen are the chef's favorite features. He also says good things about his do-everything range. "Last week I had mushrooms sautéing, a gratin in the oven, a steak grilling, water going to steam the asparagus, a double boiler on for hollandaise, and a cobbler in the other oven. For one meal, I was using practically the entire stove."

Such ambitious meal preparation is appropriate for a chef who has consistently challenged himself to master all areas of cooking. Terrance says he knew, "probably when I was in 10th grade that I wanted to be a chef." His family didn't have enough money to send him to culinary school. "But I was a hard worker and I had a passion for it, so it's where I ended up," he says. "Every place I worked, I set up my own apprenticeship program. I made sure I worked at

Above, The island's deep basket drawers are perfect for onions, garlic, shallots, potatoes…and crayons. **Right,** Julie transferred the luscious-looking fruit in her sofa fabric to hand-painted tiles. Throughout the kitchen, these custom-made Anne Sacks tiles provide colorful accents.

Left, Julie lends a hand with the cheese tray. The Brennans wanted enough counter space for family and friends to gather together and to cook together. The limestone, which acquires a patina with use, makes a great countertop and provides just the right touch for their country kitchen.

everything—*garde manger, saucier,* pastry, butcher. And if I didn't get the experience at one job, I'd fill in on my off hours at another restaurant."

After a few years as executive sous-chef at a large hotel in Washington, D.C., Terrance was in line for an executive chef job when he realized that he didn't want it. "I decided that I wanted to be my own boss, to own my own restaurant, and I wanted it to be so good that I could take weekends off, because I wanted a real family life." To get the experience he needed, Terrance went to New York. After working at New York's Le Cirque for 2½ years, Terrance spent 1½ years in France and Italy, apprenticing at such three-star restaurants as Taillevent, Tour d'Argent, and with Roger Verge at Moulin de Mougins.

Back in New York, Terrance launched Picholine in 1993 as a neighborhood bistro serving rustic Mediterranean cuisine. He and Julie immediately began to refine the concept, changing and upgrading a bit at a time, adding Christofle silver, exquisite fabrics, Limoges china, crystal chandeliers, and a greatly expanded wine list. The food evolved, too. Now a cheese cave stores 50 different cheeses, which are dispensed with a flourish by a maître fromager. Picholine's classic cuisine includes wild mushroom and duck risotto with white truffle oil, and delicious signature dishes such as poached halibut with roasted beets, wilted spinach, and oestra caviar sauce.

At home, the Brennans have upgraded and refined, too. "When we decided to remodel and improve our kitchen space, we made it as nice as possible because we want to spend a lot of time in there as a family, enjoying each other's company and cooking together."

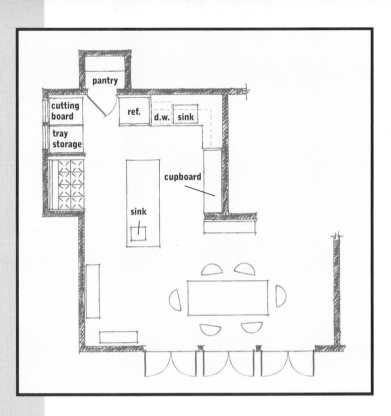

In the floor plan, the following labels appear:

- pantry
- cutting board
- ref.
- d.w.
- sink
- tray storage
- cupboard
- sink

"I know how expensive it is to have custom cabinets made. It's cheaper to buy antiques."

Nancy Oakes Bruce Aidells

Boulevard
Aidells'
Sausage Co.

Nancy Oakes is chef and co-owner of Boulevard, ranked the top San Francisco restaurant by Zagat's survey in 1998 and 1999. Food and Wine *named her one of the 10 Best New Chefs in 1993; she was a Beard Foundation nominee for Best California Chef in 1998 and 1999. Bruce Aidells owns Aidells' Sausage Company in San Leandro, California. He has contributed to nine cookbooks, including* The Complete Meat Cookbook *and the recently updated* Joy of Cooking.

Opposite, *Preparing Bruce's delicious sausages for supper.*

Nancy Oakes and Bruce Aidells are known as hospitable, friendly sorts, so it stands to reason that their kitchen is homey, warm, and welcoming. The space is also practical, well equipped, and laid out for professional-level cooking, because that's what they do, on the job and off. Like their marriage, the kitchen is a successful mix of two personalities.

Drawers in the island have cut-down fronts for visibility and racks for hard-to-store items. The Victorian English armoire beyond was originally a linen press. Pull-out shelves store dishes and glassware. The island's French blue harmonizes with the Turkish rugs. The butcher block overhang makes a handy niche for a garbage can.

Nancy and Bruce married in 1990 and set up housekeeping in Bruce's woodsy Arts and Crafts home nestled on a Kensington, California, hillside. Four years later, the couple decided it was time to remodel their house, even though they were busy at work—Boulevard, Nancy's San Francisco restaurant, was packing them in, and Aidells' Sausage Company was, too, producing more than 50,000 pounds of sausage a week.

Their plans called for upgrading the charming but small house by adding a new bath and bedroom upstairs and connecting three tiny rooms on the main floor to create an open, L-shaped kitchen and dining area. Three sets of double French doors would lead to a deck with sweeping views of San Francisco Bay. Once they had their basic building ideas in order, however, the couple sensed it would be best to split the decision-making. As Bruce says, "We couldn't work together on anything of this scale." Nancy laughs, "I took the upstairs remodel, and let Bruce have the kitchen."

Because he was in charge of kitchen planning, Bruce—co-author of *The Complete Meat Cookbook*—built the kitchen around a huge butcher block he had "lucked into" 15 years earlier. A local butcher shop that was going out of business offered the block for $100. "You can't get boards that big and substantial anymore. It was a bear getting it in here, but I made sure I wasn't home when they hauled it up the hill."

The 4-in.-thick block made a hefty 3-ft. by 8-ft. center island with a prep sink at one end. Beneath the butcher block, Bruce installed drawers with cut-down fronts. "I wanted to have the advantage of open shelving, where you can see what you've got, but still be able to pull the drawers out to get to what's at the back." Some of the drawers are extra deep for storing large pots, grinders, sausage stuffers, and bowls.

To keep cabinetry to a minimum, Bruce and Nancy bought a pair of antique oak armoires. "I know how expensive it is to have custom cabinets made," Bruce says. "It's cheaper to buy antiques, and then you have something of value, too. You can't beat the vintage looks and that patina of age."

Acquiring antiques, though, meant that any new cabinetry needed to harmonize. For a bank of cabinets under the cleanup sink, Nancy wanted old-looking oak. "Our cabinetmaker worked hard to match the look of that armoire, and he succeeded amazingly well," Bruce says.

Topping the oak cabinetry, stainless-steel counters with a raised edge and a backsplash with a vertical-stripe pattern make a practical yet pretty cleanup area. Bruce designed the deep, custom-made sink to handle his largest pots. "I used to wash big things in a little-bitty home sink, and basically what you'd end up with is a lot of water in your lap," he explains. In the Oakes-Aidells kitchen, washing up and loading the KitchenAid dishwasher is a neater affair.

Nancy wanted open shelves over the sink for storing her collection of hand-painted Italian plates and platters. This arrangement makes it a snap to put the dishes away and also creates a highly decorative display; it's Nancy's favorite thing about the kitchen.

The stainless-steel KitchenAid refrigerator ended up between the sink and pantry door. Bruce calls that placement "our biggest layout dilemma. But once I decided I wanted the big armoire over closer to the dining table, and the range was for sure going along that outside wall opposite, the refrigerator had to go where it is."

Beyond the refrigerator and pantry Bruce has his big range. "That's my 'industrial' corner," he says. "It's exactly the installation you'd have in a commercial kitchen, stainless-steel-lined walls and everything, except I should have had the hood made a little bit deeper." The range is a commercial six-burner Montague Grizzly with a custom grill and two ovens—one convection and one for roasting.

A butcher block–topped rolling unit with slide-in sheet pans resides next to the range. "People never plan on where to put the hot stuff just out of the oven," according to Bruce. "That's what these racks are for."

The kitchen feature Bruce likes best is the industrial-strength pot rack. "This thing is into the joists," he laughs. "It would hold me and a few of my friends hanging up there. We put a lot of thought into the lights because of the pot rack, though," Bruce recalls. "We tried to design the lighting so that it would illuminate the work surfaces and not just be hitting the ceiling above the pots." Nancy likes that all the lights are on dimmer switches, to change the ambiance when food goes on the table.

Bruce sums up: "The kitchen works really well. We set it up the way we did because when we have people over, we both cook." The couple planned the space on the "outside" of the island to be wide enough for friends to gather in the kitchen but away from the big range. "You always need to account for guests," Nancy says.

At Boulevard, Nancy built her reputation on fabulous, home-style food and treating her guests well. "The hospitality level is very high there," says Bruce. "The cooks hate it when she's anywhere near the

Open shelves above the cleanup sink provide attractive storage for Nancy's collection of colorful, hand-painted Italian plates. Under-sink cabinets are new oak, carefully stained to match the antique armoire. Bruce's custom-made, deep, 20-in. by 28-in. stainless-steel sink accommodates even the largest pots.

Above, The L-shaped dining area and kitchen is a great place for entertaining. Bruce says the kitchen is "extremely homey—that's what we like."

Left, Bruce designed an ample spice rack because, "when you cook food from all over the place, you end up with lots of different spices and condiments."

line, because she starts making these promises to people for food that's not even on the menu. She takes care of everybody."

Nancy grew up in the business. Her mother owned the Bluebird Restaurant, a Carmel, California, eatery with a menu straight out of her native New England: crab cakes, lobster stew, fried oysters, clam chowder, and Yankee pot roast. The down-home fare hinted at the earthy, honest food Nancy today serves.

After earning her bachelor's degree from San Francisco's Art Institute, Nancy decided against a career in art and took up cooking in the commune where she lived. She also "worked the front of the house" at several upscale restaurants in San Francisco. In her first kitchen job, at a dockside joint called the Barnacle, Nancy served up hearty meals to "longshoremen types." From the Barnacle, she moved on to Pat O'Shea's Mad Hatter, an Irish sports bar. "My first 10 years in cooking were basically in dives," Nancy says, but the experience was invaluable. In 1988, a small space became available next door to O'Shea's, and Nancy grabbed it. She turned it into L'Avenue, her own 54-seat restaurant; it attracted rave reviews and a loyal local following, including a sausage maker named Bruce Aidells and restaurant impresario Pat Kuleto.

When Kuleto sampled Nancy's corn and lobster fritters and pan-roasted pork tenderloin, he wanted to open a much larger restaurant to showcase her cooking. Boulevard opened in 1993 and was chosen the favorite San Francisco restaurant by Zagat's 1998 and 1999 surveys. It routinely gets 1,000 reservation requests a day for its 160 seats.

Boulevard's offerings include glazed sweetbreads with porcini mushroom and fava bean panzanella and sweet onion marmalade; wood oven–roasted rack of lamb served with spring green garlic mashed potatoes and grilled artichoke hearts, watercress salad, mint vinaigrette, and red wine sauce; and Meyer lemon caramel icebox cake served with blueberry-huckleberry compote. Which may be why, when asked by the *San Francisco Chronicle*'s Karola Sackel, "What foods make you happy?" Bruce responded by saying, "Anything my wife cooks—no really—and I love homey desserts."

Bruce got into cooking at graduate school, working at a little restaurant on campus at the University of California at Santa Cruz. But cooking did not become Bruce's vocation immediately. First, he finished his Ph.D. in endocrinology and went to England to spend five years in cancer research.

He likes to tell about being stuck in London with nothing to eat but "bangers and mash," that peculiar British meal of mashed potatoes and sausages. He knew he could do better, so he began to investigate sausage-making between his other experiments. The results steadily improved, and when he came back to Oakland, he continued to make sausage. Now, though, he was getting requests from a number of small delis and restaurants.

The next step from cancer researcher to "sausage king" was a job at an all-chicken restaurant in Berkeley called Poulet. He launched Aidells' Sausage Company in 1983, and by 1998 it had become a $10 million producer of 30 kinds of sausage, including chicken-apple, Cajun tasso, and smoked turkey-chicken-artichoke. Bruce also has nine cookbooks to his credit, and was a contributing editor for the meat and chicken sections of the recent *Joy of Cooking* update. Late 1998 saw the release of his encyclopedic, well-received book, *The Complete Meat Cookbook,* a project he worked on with collaborator Denis Kelly.

What's next for Bruce and Nancy? Without a doubt it will involve great kitchens and good cooking, mixed with ample measures of wit, warmth, and enthusiasm—an old Oakes-Aidells family recipe.

A commercial butcher block–topped rolling unit with slide-in sheet pans resides by the range. Bruce and Nancy's knives are in a wooden holder attached to the butcher block.

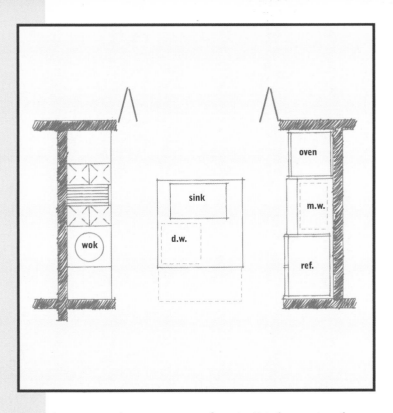

The wok is very hot, very fast. It has to be,
for Chinese cooking. It's impossible if the
heat isn't high enough because everything
would get watery, soggy."

Cecilia Chiang

Cecilia Chiang likes to eat simply at home. "I might steam green beans, a little sesame seed oil, and soy sauce. A few noodles. That's all." That may be all, but you can bet that those beans with Chinese noodles would be perfect. This legendary San Francisco restaurateur and chef has based her career, and her life, on hard work and attention to detail. When—at age 74—Cecilia came out of retirement to consult on opening Betelnut, a ground-breaking pan-Asian restaurant, critic Patricia Unterman gave it three stars and wrote, "Cecilia Chiang is on the floor every night, impossibly picky, ever watchful. The only way the staff can survive her is by getting it right."

Thirty years ago, Cecilia bought her home on San Francisco Bay, just north of the city. The house was very well situated, according to the ancient Chinese principles of *feng shui,* but the kitchen was not "right." Cecilia immediately set about making it so. She recalls, "Although this is a large, comfortable house, its kitchen is very small." Since the previous owner had five children, there was a long eating bar between the kitchen and family room, with stools on the family room side where the kids had their meals. In the kitchen, an electric cooktop with four burners sat just below the bar. Cecilia says, "Probably the mother just stood in one spot and cooked and then served everything up on the bar. Only one person could fit in the kitchen!" Worse yet, on one side of the tiny, 10-sq.-ft. room, a solid wall blocked access to the dining room. Cecilia explains, "To go to the dining room from the kitchen, you had to make a little tour

through a hallway or walk the other way across the deck. It was really not a very good setup."

Her first step was to remove the eating counter and take down the opposite wall between kitchen and dining room. In short order, Cecilia had created a pass-through kitchen that, though still small, was now wide open to both the family room and dining room. She planned to put her cooktop and wok on one side wall, with a Sub-Zero refrigerator and two Thermador wall ovens on the other. A compact, maple butcher block–topped island with inset sink and dishwasher would become the kitchen's centerpiece.

The island has worked out well. Its top is slightly over 4 ft. on a side, but Cecilia designed a hinged leaf that adds another 2 ft. "If I do some serious cooking or entertain my friends, we can all work here when the leaf is up," she says. Cecilia has taught countless

Opposite, The maple butcher block island works well for food prep and cleanup. When Cecilia needs a bit more room, she extends the island's hinged leaf. A skylight above brings natural light into the tiny kitchen. **Left,** The stainless-steel cover over the wok closes to make additional work surface. The tile backsplash extends up to the hood for easy cleaning. **Below,** Cecilia wok-cooks savory bok choy and mushrooms.

Chinese cooking classes in the small kitchen, using the island as an efficient, central work space. She likes to eat right in the kitchen. "If I'm at home by myself, I can just pull up a little stool and have my supper here."

On one side of the island, Cecilia installed an oversize, stainless-steel Elkay double sink with a Delta faucet. She especially likes her cutting board, which slides over one side of the sink; it's easy to chop, then scrape vegetable leavings right into the disposal. Cecilia is careful to point out that the island's chopping block top must be kept oiled—especially around the sink, where splashed water could ruin the unsealed maple. An instant-hot-water faucet set into the island is perfect for making tea. A KitchenAid dishwasher in the island completes the picture.

Directly over the island, Cecilia added a skylight that is just the size of the chopping block below. She wanted to bring natural light into the dark kitchen, which is the only room in the house that's not wide open to expansive views of San Francisco Bay. Track lighting around the edges of the skylight illuminates the area after dark. Below the skylight, Cecilia installed a big pot rack because, "this kitchen doesn't have enough cabinets for all the pots and woks and steamers you need for Chinese cooking."

Another prerequisite for cooking Chinese style is very high heat. Cecilia replaced the electric cooktop with four large gas burners and a grill, which she says is good for fish. Next to the cooktop is a custom-made wok. Cecilia explains, "Because the space was so small, I had to design this wok myself. I couldn't find a premade unit that would fit." For extra fire power, the gas line is big—almost the

The ample, built-in wok is essential to Cecilia's kitchen. Its large gas supply line ensures very high heat, so vegetables cook quickly. Spices are kept in the drawers below the wok, for easy access. Cecilia prepares simple dishes at home, but the results are always spectacular.

same size as the line for a commercial installation. "This wok is very hot, very fast. It has to be, for Chinese cooking. It's impossible if the heat isn't high enough because everything would get watery, soggy." When it's not in use, a stainless-steel lid covers the wok to yield additional work surface. Cecilia's powerful, custom-made hood with its subtle Asian motif extends over both cooktop and wok. Drawers for Cecilia's spices, oils, and condiments are positioned just below the wok for quick access while cooking.

Cecilia wanted the kitchen to be very simple, clean, and unclut-tered, because it is wide open to the dining room, where she likes to display her priceless art: antique ginger jars, Ming Dynasty paintings, "forbidden stitch" tapestries, and a Coromandel screen. She thought the kitchen should recede visually into the background. That's why she chose plain brown tile in the same size and tone for floor, coun-tertops, and backsplashes. The backsplash tile extends up to the hood to facilitate cleaning behind cooktop and wok because oil is often used in wok cooking, and it inevitably spatters. Unadorned white cabinets without knobs or pulls provide a uniform background for the room. When Cecilia entertains in her elegant dining room, she can close off the kitchen with folding, louvered doors. She uses her massive, carved rosewood dining table for Chinese banquets—a suc-cession of up to 20 separate hot and cold dishes—but never rice. "At a banquet you don't serve rice—that's for everyday," Cecilia says.

Cecilia was born into a wealthy, land-owning Mandarin family in Beijing. But her carefree, privileged upbringing among 11 brothers and sisters soon turned bleak with World War II and the Japanese occupation of China. The family's land was confiscated and they were turned out of their ancestral home. In 1943, Cecilia and her number five sister decided to flee to Free China. Disguised as peasants, with gold pieces sewn into their clothing, the frightened young women walked more than 1,000 miles to safety in Chungking. It took them five months.

After the war, Cecilia and her new husband were posted to Japan, where he worked for the Chinese Mission. "I didn't know how to cook at all. I had never been allowed in the kitchen as a girl; servants cooked. And there was no Chinese food to be had in Japan. I didn't like the local food—all that raw fish!—so I had to learn how to prepare the dishes I wanted. You always long for your own food." Quickly adapting, Cecilia learned her way around a kitchen and then opened a Chinese restaurant—a rarity in Tokyo in 1951.

Seven years later, she emigrated to the United States and, in 1962, opened her first restaurant in San Francisco. The original 65-seat Mandarin on Polk Street had an inauspicious beginning. In partnership with three friends, and as the only one who spoke English, Cecilia negotiated the restaurant's lease. Her partners backed out at the last minute and Cecilia was left with the space— and her new restaurant. "It was by mistake," she says, "but it was supposed to be, I guess." Cecilia describes the staffing: "One cook, one kitchen assistant, one dishwasher. No janitor. I was the janitor, the receptionist, the busboy. I did all jobs. That's how I learned." She was also working hard at home, caring for—and cooking for—her two children. Much later, she recognizes this as a pivotal time. "My whole life had changed, from not being allowed in the kitchen as a girl to doing every job in the kitchen. But I couldn't have succeeded if I didn't like it. The first thing is that you must enjoy what you are doing. Then you have to do it over and over."

Left, A steaming basket is placed over water in a wok. Vinegars, oils, and bottled sauces are handy to the cooktop. **Above,** Whole steamed rock cod with scallions, cilantro, and fresh ginger awaits lucky guests.

Friends in the restaurant business advised Cecilia to offer familiar Cantonese dishes such as chop suey or egg foo yung at her new place. "But I didn't know Cantonese food at all, I'll be very honest. All I knew was Northern food, Mandarin, so that's what I cooked." It was the right choice. The dining public immediately took to her rarified Mongolian lamb, minced squab, and kung pao shrimp. In 1968 the Mandarin moved to a serenely luxurious 300-seat space in Ghirardelli Square, where it reigned supreme until Cecilia retired in 1991.

The retiree was to enjoy her leisure for just a few years before being drafted to help establish a new restaurant, the pan-Asian phenomenon, Betelnut. Betelnut is a "pejiu wu," or beer house, that serves an array of dishes from many Asian locales. Shortly after it opened, Michael Bauer wrote in the *San Francisco Chronicle,* "The strength of the menu is in the Chinese selections. Cecilia Chiang, who transformed Chinese food in the United States...greets guests and is responsible for many of the stellar dishes," including velvety minced chicken served in lettuce cups and Madame Chiang's red-cooked pork.

Betelnut's kitchen is very small and open, surrounded by an L-shaped counter with 15 of the hottest seats in town. "That was my idea," Cecilia says. "These days, a lot of single people go out to eat alone, and you don't want to sit at a table by yourself, so it's good to have the counter. You can talk to the person sitting next to you, or you can watch the cooks. I always wanted to have a restaurant like that."

At 78, Cecilia is still generating ideas, and going strong. She recently returned from a three-week tour of the "Silk Road" with friends, and is consulting on yet another new San Francisco restaurant. She regularly goes to Los Angeles to visit with her son, Philip, who is the food consultant for the popular P. F. Chang restaurants across the country.

When she's in the Bay Area, Cecilia makes time to see her daughter, May—owner of Kite, a San Francisco restaurant—and to enjoy her home, which she says is "very practical. The house is right on the water, and the deck is good for barbecues in the late summer and fall."

So why did this world-class chef and restaurateur buy a house with such a small kitchen? "I knew I could make it right," she says with a radiant smile, "and the *feng shui* was unbelievably good."

Opposite, Cecilia opened up the wall between her kitchen and dining room. A rosewood table accommodates family banquets; the carved mantelpiece beyond displays a Goddess of Mercy sculpture. **Above,** A Coromandel cabinet, inlaid with mother of pearl, holds antique dishes. **Left,** Cecilia's deck is right on San Francisco Bay.

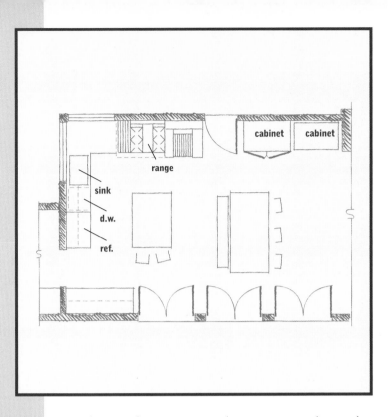

Robert Del Grande's special brand of "New Texas Cuisine" has had a profound influence on the Houston restaurant scene. The fine-dining Café Annie is consistently voted a favorite destination, and Gourmet magazine rates it one of America's Top Tables. To boot, Robert was named Best Southwest Chef by the James Beard Foundation in 1992. Now, Houston—and Dallas—diners can also experience Robert's Taco Milagro and Rio Ranch restaurants and his more casual Café Express eateries.

Opposite, Robert's kitchen is a natural gathering place.

"I always say that if you can have one hand on the refrigerator door and one hand stirring a pot on the stove, you're set."

Robert Del Grande

Five years ago, Southwestern food pioneer Robert Del Grande was lined up to appear on Julia Child's *Cooking with Master Chefs* TV series. Assured that the shows would be shot in the chefs' restaurant kitchens, Robert and his wife, Mimi, began remodeling their newly purchased Houston home. The minute their house was totally gutted, Robert learned the show would be filmed there. The camera crew arrived to a stripped-down Del Grande abode—no furniture, no paint, no bathrooms, very few walls—but the kitchen was completely finished, stocked, equipped, decorated, and ready to go. "Basically, this kitchen began life as a TV studio," Robert says with a grin.

Above, *Robert grills all kinds of meats and vegetables on his custom indoor grill. It has a Texas limestone surround and heavy-duty iron inset with doors for safety. The grill is vented by a custom hood that extends across the Thermador range as well.*

Opposite, *Colorful masks of Bacchus, painted Italian jars, larger-than-life ceramic artichokes, and a carved wooden strip from India decorate the cooking area. Robert has collected copper pots since his college days.*

Robert and Mimi had wanted a house close to their hot-as-a-pistol Houston restaurant, Café Annie—one of 11 restaurants in the Del Grande corral. They also wanted a suitable place to raise their daughter, Tessa, now in elementary school. Their third criterion was to find a house with space that could be opened into one large kitchen, dining, and living room. Mimi soon found a house that filled the bill. Though unassuming and "ranch-y," it was in a well-located neighborhood of much larger homes, had a huge backyard with mature trees, and presented a long roof line to the street. Mimi brought Robert by to see it, saying, "Don't look at the house, look at its potential." He was sold.

Working with Houston architect Joe Milton, the couple first consolidated the central core of their boxy home. Robert recalls that the house "had that 1950s kind of compartmentalized-by-function layout. You know, there was a little sewing room with walls, a little breakfast room with walls, a little kitchen with walls. Every activity had its narrowly defined space." The interior walls came down while Robert worked on the layout for the kitchen/great room area. Placed at one end, the kitchen "works really well, because it kind of lets the spirit define the space. If it's a more food-oriented event, the kitchen will get bigger and bigger. And if there's more going on that's not related to food, the kitchen seems to shrink back this way," Robert says. For Christmas dinner, the entire space is given over to food: A long table seating 20 people stretches the length of the room so the whole clan can eat together.

While addressing the space overall, Robert also carefully planned the details. His first step was to position appliances, sink, and food preparation areas in an efficient L-shaped work space with a Sub-Zero refrigerator, Bosch dishwasher, and custom-made stainless-steel sink aligned along one side of the L. The Thermador range occupies the other. The compact, almost square, island with butcher block top fits into the L and conveniently serves both sides. Robert explains, "In a way this kitchen has a restaurant setup. There are 'stations' for various cooking activities. You especially want spots to put things down without taking a lot of extra steps." In homes, as in restaurants, "too big a kitchen is just as bad as too small a kitchen," Robert says. "Sometimes after you work in a big kitchen you're really

exhausted from all the wasted movement. That one extra step 500 times a day will really wear you out. I always say that if you can have one hand on the refrigerator door and one hand stirring a pot on the stove, you're set."

Robert chose a domestic Thermador range because he doesn't believe professional models are well enough insulated for the cook's comfort in a home kitchen—especially in a climate like Houston's. The range he selected is "plenty powerful but also has a great low simmer," says Robert. The Del Grandes like the way it looks, too. Robert says, "The finish and trim details are nice; this range is very residential in feel. Aesthetics are important when your kitchen is open to the primary living space."

With the Thermador's six burners, two ovens, and a griddle, you'd think that the chef had enough cooking options, but Robert set his heart on extending the "hot line" with an indoor wood-burning grill—this is Texas, after all. Although Mimi wanted Robert to "just grill in

the backyard like everybody else," Robert knew "you can't orchestrate the meal if you have to run in and out between the kitchen and the patio." He pushed for the indoor grill and eventually "she let me do it," he says. A custom-made stainless-steel hood extends over both range and grill.

The heavy-duty grill with handsome, warm-toned limestone surround and specially designed metal door is good looking and great for cooking. Robert enjoys grilling vegetables, chicken, steak, and hamburgers on it: "You can even manage a whole leg of lamb, if you're game to turn it over 'Renaissance-style'—by hand." Robert

deliberately matched the height of the grill with that of the range because, "When I take something out of the oven and need a place to set it down, I use the grill, and vice versa; the stove top works great to hold foods that are just off the grill." Robert believes that many kitchens have adequate space for equipment and ingredients that are "put away," but not for those being used.

While at the hot line, Robert can turn around and gather his ready-to-go ingredients from the island or chop on the maple butcher block island top. The island also makes a convenient place for plating food. Robert likes a work island where cooks can face each other and talk while they're working, having learned in professional kitchens that countertops facing walls are not congenial to ensemble cooking.

Robert and Mimi wanted a microwave for occasional use. They tucked theirs into an opening in the island. Also under the island top is a handy built-in rack that stores cutting boards. The island provides a good place for sitting, too; twin slat-backed wooden stools with comfortable cushions make an ideal spot for Robert and Mimi to read the newspaper while drinking their morning coffee.

Lighting in the kitchen is as important for cooking as for reading. Recessed spotlights evenly spaced throughout the kitchen are on two circuits, and all the lights are on rheostats. "I love rheostats," Robert says, "I prefer to cook in softer light—it can be so harsh in a restau-

rant. You do need true light, so you can see the color of the food, but it doesn't have to be all that bright."

Robert values the fact that he has a "cool kitchen"—thanks to central air-conditioning, a high-powered hood, and tile floor. "I'm interested in the management of heat," he says. "They say, 'If you can't stand the heat, get out of the kitchen.' Well, maybe kitchens shouldn't be hot; you can't be very social in a kitchen if it's too warm, and our kitchen is designed for socializing." The one thing Robert might change about his kitchen is to have high and low speeds on the hood vent instead of just high. The venting action is a little loud, he says. By the time he thought of it, though, the wiring was installed.

Robert certainly brought his professional cooking expertise to the Del Grande home kitchen, but neither he nor Mimi wanted it to look

like a restaurant space. Mimi and her sister, Candice Schiller—who decorated the Del Grandes' restaurants—quickly went to work finishing the room in a *simpatico* style that artfully mixes Southwest with a dash of European tradition. For the floor, they chose terra-cotta Mexican *Saltillo* tiles because they're easy to keep clean and are cool underfoot. Mimi liked the fact that the tiles need just a little wax and damp mopping for upkeep. Glazed, hand-painted Mexican tile provides bright accents on the countertops and backsplashes. A soft moss-green wash applied to the cabinets and island creates a rustic finish that lets the wood's grain show through.

Open-shelf cabinets display the Del Grandes' favorite painted ceramic dishes from Italy and Mexico. Other ceramics bought on the couple's travels—such as a collection of Venetian masks of Bacchus and another of larger-than-life, white artichokes—add wit and character to the kitchen. "We like to have things around us that remind us of wonderful times we've had," Mimi says.

The couple's mesquite dining table was custom-made. In addition to being closely associated with Texas, mesquite is a very hard wood and requires no maintenance, Mimi says. With formal, high-backed chairs on one side and a picnic bench on the other, the table continues the kitchen's down-home-mixed-with-classics theme. Decorative touches include whimsical fruit and flower garlands draped above the windows, a carved strip of wood over the range and grill—"it frames Robert's area," says Mimi, and, of course, a treasure trove of copper pots.

Opposite, Three sets of oversize French doors open to the large patio and backyard, where Tessa likes to play with friends. High-backed wooden stools at the island make a good spot for morning coffee. *Left,* A microwave tucked into the island is most often used to melt butter for Sunday pancake breakfasts. *Above,* A convenient rack for storing cutting boards was built into the island.

Robert grew up in San Francisco, graduated from the University of San Francisco, and went on to the University of California at Riverside to earn his Ph.D. in biochemistry. Although he didn't know it at the time, Robert now says that moving into a house with two other graduate students was the birth of his career in cooking—rather than biochemistry. As he tells it, the threesome decided to take turns making dinner. The first two nights featured specialties "from their moms' 3x5 cards—you know, the kind of recipe where dry oatmeal is used as a meat loaf extender. On the third day, when it was my turn, I took a big roasting chicken, quartered it up, put potatoes

and onions in it, and basted it until it was about perfect. They were delirious. They thought it was the best thing they'd ever eaten," Robert remembers. "And in their delirium they said, 'Why don't you do all the cooking and we'll clean up?' So, for the next five years, I cooked and they washed the dishes." And a chef was born.

When Robert finished graduate school in 1981, he followed his girlfriend, Mimi, to Houston. There, he worked in the kitchen at Café Annie, a six-month-old restaurant owned by Mimi's sister, Candice, and brother-in-law, Lonnie Schiller. Robert explains, "I'd been going to school for nine years straight, and I was burned out. I wanted to have a little fun." Eighteen years later, that "little bit of fun" has resulted in a veritable dynasty of Del Grande-Schiller restaurants: the fine-dining flagship, Café Annie, Taco Milagro, Rio Ranch, and eight upscale, fast-food Café Express restaurants in Houston and Dallas.

By serving such dishes-with-a-twist as goat cheese and black bean terrine, Southwestern shrimp grilled in corn husks, and pork loin with pumpkin seed sauce, Café Annie has earned Zagat's vote as Houston's favorite restaurant for an astounding seven years running. Although Robert steadfastly resists labels—"I cook what I cook. If you grill fresh fish with lemon and cilantro, what else would you call it?"—he is often credited with fathering the branch of Southwest cookery now known as "New Texas Cuisine."

As much as Robert savors his executive chef role, he enjoys cooking simple foods at home. "It's how I relax," he explains. "There's no waiter here saying, 'Where's this. Where's that? What's going on?'" Robert also says he has learned a lot by cooking for his daughter, who prefers pared-down dishes with a limited number of ingredients.

All in all, Robert Del Grande's haute-on-the-range cooking mixes bright, bold, border flavors with a classic sensibility. His home kitchen does the same.

Opposite, A closet with deep shelves offers storage for large platters and other serving pieces. A picnic bench mixes with more traditional chairs to offer informal seating at the custom-made mesquite dining table. *Below,* Garlands over the windows were created by Whitney Bishop, who arranges flowers for the Del Grande restaurants. Colorful dishes sit in open cabinets.

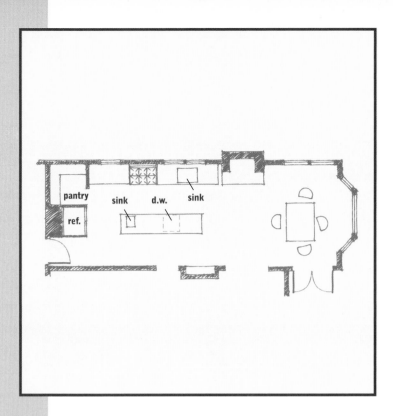

pantry
ref.
sink
d.w.
sink

"My kitchen is set up for cooking from scratch because I like to get to the bottom of things, to understand the structure—whether it's food, music, or writing."

Paul Bertolli

Oliveto

Paul Bertolli is chef and co-owner of Oliveto in Oakland, California. His rustic yet refined Italian cooking earned him a 1998 James Beard Foundation nomination as Best Chef in California. Paul first attracted attention for his culinary prowess at Chez Panisse, where he was chef of the downstairs restaurant for 10 years. In 1988 he wrote Chez Panisse Cooking *with Alice Waters.*

Opposite, *Linda helps Paul prepare vegetables for the grill.*

Paul Bertolli takes an intuitive approach to cooking. He studies, analyzes, gets to the bottom of—*really understands and responds to*—his ingredients, and then translates that information into utterly simple, unforgettable food. When designing his newly remodeled home kitchen, he took that same approach.

Four years ago, Paul and his wife, Linda, bought a charming—albeit small and unimproved—home in the Berkeley, California, hills. The couple needed a place close to Oliveto, Paul's top-notch restaurant, and within commuting distance of Linda's marketing job. Though the house was tiny, it came with a large lot and a quiet, woodsy location with broad views of San Francisco Bay. The kitchen was at the back of the house, tucked into a southwest-facing hillside. Paul immediately envisioned his own little bit of Tuscany: a neatly terraced vegetable garden, fruit orchard, wine cellar, outdoor bread oven, and meat-curing room (for salami, prosciutto, and the occasional wild boar Paul bags in Sonoma County) all fitting into the up-sloping landscape.

Working with architect Timothy Gray, the Bertollis spent 2½ years planning their extensive remodel. The work included raising ceilings, adding rooms upstairs, and creating a kitchen that would be at the center of their home. Although a major construction project can be stressful ("suddenly it's not about a house, but about how well you get along," Paul says), the venture was a runaway success. "We actually had a good time with it," says Paul, and the new kitchen is everything they planned it to be.

It's a long, narrow space—11 ft. by 37 ft.—straightforward and harmonious. Clean lines, complementary materials, subtle colors, and a simple linear arrangement make for a pleasant room that's set up for serious cooking.

For the kitchen layout, Paul recalls, "We said, 'Here's what we've got, so how can we fit in what we want and need?'" At only 11 ft. wide, the room would not comfortably accommodate counters along both long walls in addition to an island. Instead, Paul positioned the range, sink, and cook-in fireplace on one side of the room. He left the facing wall free except for a built-in dish cabinet and doorways. The result is an efficient, spacious work area with good circulation and enough elbow room for a group of cooks. "My kitchen is set up for cooking from scratch," Paul says. "I like to get to the bottom of things, to understand the structure, the 'gist'—whether it's food or music or a piece of writing."

Next, Paul turned his attention to the heart of the kitchen, a rustic but elegant cook-in fireplace. "I'm kind of a primitivist when it comes to this stuff," Paul says. "I'd like to dig a hole in the ground and build a fire and turn meat by hand over it every night, if I could. That's not really feasible with modern life, but I try to design my cooking space so that my food tastes as if that's just what has happened."

For cooked-over-the-coals flavor, Paul's fireplace has a custom-made rotisserie. Its spring-loaded spit is easy to slide into position

or take off the fire. Paul says he prefers to burn old grapevines because the embers are so hot. He also uses oak and almond woods. Paul advises adding a little green wood to the blaze, because the extra smoke it produces flavors the food.

Paul's rotisserie has two drives. He can cook a large roast such as a pork shoulder on the main horizontal spit and, at the same time, hang small birds such as quail or squab, roasting them on a vertical axis. The rotisserie's motor is outside the house, so that using the device makes virtually no sound in the kitchen. Paul cooks flat cuts of meat or fish on a Tuscan grill laid directly over the fire.

Positioned across from a 5-ft.-wide opening to the dining room, the simple yet dramatic raised fireplace makes a focal point for that room as well. Its beautifully crafted concrete hearth has crisp beveled edges and provides wood storage below. The upper surfaces of the fireplace are finished with integral-color plaster, for a "European" feel. A hand-made mantelpiece tops the fireplace opening. Fashioned from rough-hewn white oak and supported by hand-forged bronze pieces, the mantel seems at once antique and au courant.

Angelo Garro, a San Francisco metal artist, made the mantel's supports as well as the pot rack and countrified bronze "candelier"

A convenient, built-in cherry wood "vitrine" holds delicate stemware. French doors in the dining room open to the patio and Paul's hillside vegetable garden.

over the table. The pot rack was designed so that Paul and Linda wouldn't have pots dangling in their faces; both are tall (6 ft. 4 in. and 5 ft. 11 in.). In another move to accommodate their height, the kitchen ceiling was lifted to 9 ft. "Anything less would feel really low to me," Paul says.

Their height also figured in the couple's cabinet decisions. "We didn't want any upper cabinets," says Linda, "because if you're tall you can't really use a counter with cabinets over it." Paul adds, "But the main reason for not having overhead cabinets is that it allows us to have all these big window openings. We have nice, natural surroundings, and we wanted to enjoy them."

For work surfaces, Paul says, "I like to spread out when I'm cooking, to see everything and have it in close proximity to the range, but not right next to it. The island that I can just turn around to is perfect." He plans to add a butcher block–topped table on wheels, which will be parked at the end of the island. It will be used as a surface for rolling out pasta or—placed by the fireplace—as a carving table for meat coming off the spit.

Although, as Paul states, "This is a real simple kitchen," he and Linda chose the materials with great care. The flooring is 12-in.-square Italian ceramic tile. Paul says, "We went over the various possibilities for softer surfaces, like wood, but we felt that since we were going to be spending so much time in here doing a lot of cooking and 'messing up,' that a hard, cleanable surface was the best alternative." The tile was laid with very thin grout joints, again for ease in cleaning. Paul and Linda love the tile's color—a terra-cotta shade that complements the warm cherry wood cabinets, soft butter yellow walls, and brown-tone "Giallo Veneziano" Italian granite countertops.

The appliances mix practicality and good looks. Paul's stainless-steel, six-gas-burner Thermador range has a convection oven and a sealed top for easy cleaning. He didn't want a warming shelf over the burners. Instead, Paul says, "I decided I'd rather spend the money on a movable-arm water source over the stove, because we're always having pasta, filling huge pots of water."

The kitchen's two custom-made sinks also are stainless, but Paul says, "I would have made them out of granite if I'd had more money to throw at the project." His cleanup sink—placed under one of those

Left, Linda and Paul wanted large casement windows to bring the garden into their kitchen. *Below,* Crisply beveled edges are just part of the fireplace's craftsmanship.

wide windows—is extra deep to handle large pasta pots. The prep sink is set in one end of the island.

In the island, directly across from the cleanup sink, is the Bosch dishwasher. This arrangement makes for efficient and almost dripless cleanup. When the Bertollis open the dishwasher in the narrow space between the counter and island, the door fills the space and catches spills. Then they "just rinse and stash." Paul says the Bosch has a quick cycle and is sleek looking, "but primarily we like it because it's quiet."

Positioned below a cutout in the granite countertop is a garbage can for compostable waste. Except for the prep sink and waste cutout, the island's stone top is one seamless, uninterrupted sweep. "I really like looking at this island. It's such a wonderful, long piece of granite," Linda says.

At one end of the long kitchen, the Bertollis placed a Sub-Zero refrigerator and walk-in pantry. Because they have no overhead cabinets, the Bertollis considered the pantry a necessity. The Sub-Zero has a large refrigeration compartment over a small freezer. Paul likes the fact that separate motors run the refrigerator and freezer, which ensures that the temperatures stay even.

A sunny eating bay extends across the opposite end of the kitchen. Sitting here, Paul and Linda can gaze through double French doors to the patio, fruit trees, and vegetable garden. The bay also offers ringside seats for watching the action in the kitchen. "This is where we entertain," Linda says, "because everybody likes to watch Paul cook, and we enjoy having friends cook with us, too." Paul says the house was designed to be one big room downstairs, so people can "sort of meander through" from the living room to the dining area and kitchen. The kitchen's low-voltage lighting was designed to look good at night, Linda adds. "When we talked to our designer, Richard Cardello, he asked us what look we wanted, and we said, 'Just warmth. A golden glow.'"

Contemplating his extraordinary new kitchen, wine cave, meat-curing room, vinegar-making cellar, and vegetable garden, Paul says with a smile, "If I'm not happy now, when will I ever be?"

He grew up in Northern California's Marin County. Little in Paul's early life indicated he might choose a culinary career, except for an after-school job at the local supermarket and a large family that included some great Italian cooks and sausage makers. Music was the shy, studious boy's first love. Following years of after-school piano practice, Paul went to the University of California at Berkeley. Realizing after graduation that music would not support him, he went on an extended tour of Italy to find a new direction. There he fell in love again, this time with food.

Back in California, Paul cooked at a number of restaurants, eventually landing at Chez Panisse, Alice Waters' eminent Berkeley restaurant. He became the restaurant's chef and stayed for 10 years, establishing his reputation as a culinary maestro.

Right, The custom-made rotisserie in Paul's raised fireplace boasts two drives—to turn the horizontal spit and to rotate quail or squab hanging vertically over the fire. The motor is outside the house, so that the device makes virtually no noise in the kitchen.

Opposite, Paul loves his water source at the range. It works well for quickly filling large pots. Knives, oils and vinegars, and the all-important espresso maker are all close at hand.

In 1992, Paul took a break from cooking to pursue graduate work in medieval studies at the University of Toronto. On his return to the Bay Area, he did some restaurant consulting and a series of special dinners at Oliveto. Before long Paul had joined Oliveto's owners, Maggie and Bob Klein, as executive chef and co-owner.

Since then, Oliveto has drawn substantial praise. Its particularly Italian sensibility—starring fresh, unadorned ingredients cooked simply but perfectly—has garnered four stars (the highest rating) from *San Francisco Chronicle* food critic Michael Bauer. "Not only is Paul Bertolli producing the best Italian food in the Bay Area; I'd put his cooking up against that of anyone in the United States, or Italy for that matter," he wrote. After an impressive wood-burning rotisserie and grill was put into action at Oliveto, Patricia Unterman wrote in the San Francisco *Examiner,* "I had expected some changes on the menu, but I was blown away. The cooking was devastatingly good."

Other critics praise such dishes as radicchio and endive with a *bagna cauda,* asparagus-stuffed tortelloni, rotisserie-roasted pork, gratin of potatoes and artichokes, and broccoli à la romana. Giving vegetables their due, as is traditional in Italian cooking, diners choose their meat and vegetables separately. Each dish attests to Paul's understanding of its essence and his use of the best ingredients.

At home, the Bertollis planned their new kitchen to be open to the kitchen garden. "Food needs to be grown well and then cooked as soon after it's pulled from the ground as possible," Paul says. "That way, you taste the life of that vegetable. For me, cooking is all about sharing the life of food—respecting good ingredients. You can really taste the difference."

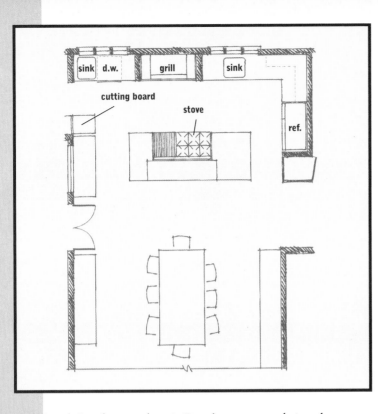

sink | d.w. | grill | sink

cutting board

stove

ref.

"I like a big kitchen, but I also need to have a beautiful view, a nice feeling. It's very important to me when I'm cooking."

**Felidia
Lidia's**

Lidia Matticchio Bastianich is often called the "First Lady" of Italian cuisine. She opened Felidia in Manhattan in 1981, co-owns Becco and Frico Bar with her son, Joseph, and recently branched out to Kansas City to launch Lidia's. Recent projects include her PBS cooking series, Lidia's Italian Table, with a companion book of the same name. Her first cookbook, La Cucina di Lidia, was published in 1990.

Opposite, Lidia loves to cook vegetables of all kinds.

Lidia Matticchio Bastianich

Lidia Bastianich understands that quality requires few embellishments. She carries out that characteristically Italian approach to food at her restaurants in Manhattan—Felidia, Becco, and Frico Bar—and at Lidia's, her newest venture, in Kansas City. And though it's far from Italy, her home kitchen overlooking Long Island Sound also abounds with Italian style.

Above, For safety, a raised counter shields the Vulcan range's powerful cooktop. The range hood also vents the grill. *Above right,* Lidia's family likes to gather in the kitchen. *Left,* Dough for squash-filled ravioli is rolled out on the granite countertop.

Life wasn't always so comfortable. In Pula, a village in the war-torn Istrian Peninsula northeast of Italy (now a part of Croatia), her family was alternately considered Italian, Austrian, and Yugoslavian as political winds shifted. They emigrated to the United States when Lidia was 12, but only after several years in a refugee camp near Trieste. At the camp, her mother, Erminia, would get up before dawn to help with the cooking; in exchange, she received an extra handful of rice for Lidia and her brother. (Forty years later, Erminia recounts with delight and gratitude their very first dinner in this country—whole roast chicken with mashed potatoes at a New York cafeteria, capped off with brightly colored Jell-O, which the kids insisted on trying.)

Lidia gravitated naturally toward cooking. Her grandmother and great aunt had grounded her in the basics of their border region cuisine. Influenced by many cultures, a cool climate, and a bounty of game and seafood, the cuisine encompassed such varied dishes as mussels in saffron broth and venison *ossobuco* with spaetzle. In New York, Lidia made the family dinner when her parents worked late. They ate well: Twelve-year-old Lidia prepared complete three-course dinners.

Although Lidia's kitchen has clean, modern lines, it also says Old World. The graceful etched art glass and tiled walls complement the granite counters and custom cherry cabinets. Etched glass doors also decorate the cabinets in the dining area. Lidia's pasta machine and cappuccino maker are at the ready.

Left, *Carrying kindling in her apron, Lidia's mother, Erminia, makes a fire in the imported Endinea grill. A rack against the back wall holds the fire until coals drop down, to be raked forward for cooking. Beneath the grill, a drawer collects ashes. The fireplace-like opening was built especially for the grill and is lined with blue-and-white painted tiles that Lidia says impart an "Italian look." Pots hang snugly against the wall, ready but not in the way.*
Above, *vegetables roast slowly on the rotisserie.*

Summer jobs during Lidia's school years included restaurant and winery jobs in Italy. So Lidia's friends and family weren't surprised when in 1971 she opened Buonavia, in Forest Hills, New York. Ten years later she sold Buonavia and a second restaurant, Villa Secondo, to fulfill her dream of owning an elegant Italian restaurant in Manhattan. She opened Felidia in an old brownstone on the Upper East Side.

After establishing Felidia, Lidia and her family bought a large, Tudor-style house on Long Island Sound. The first task was gutting the first-floor service area, which consisted of several small rooms and a narrow, interior kitchen. Lidia opened it up into one large, square room with a view, because she wanted ample space and a view of the water while she cooked. "I like a big kitchen, but I also need to have a beautiful view, a nice feeling. It's very important to me when I'm cooking," she says. The kitchen's rustic pine table seats 12 and is positioned in the center of the room, where Lidia's guests can be involved in what she's doing.

Aside from the amount of space, the most significant element of Lidia's kitchen is *la griglia.* She bought the Endinea grill in Italy to become the centerpiece of her new kitchen. Although she also has a grill outdoors, Lidia wanted all-season access to grilling, which is essential in Italian cooking. With the Endinea, the fire is made in a rack on the back wall of the grill. When the coals are ready, they are raked forward to roast bell peppers and red onions or to impart that smoky flavor to squab that slowly turns on the motorized rotisserie. A removable cover goes on after the food is in place to retain the heat and channel the smoke out the vent. The raised fireplace-like opening, built to hold the grill, was finished with rustic blue-and-white painted tiles—which are Portuguese but have an "Italian look," Lidia says. Pots and utensils hang snugly against the walls around the grill, in view but out of the way.

Directly across from the grill is Lidia's commercial Vulcan range. With its six burners, griddle, and two ovens—one regular, one convection—Lidia "can do everything." The counter behind the range is raised about a foot, to shield guests from the high-powered cooktop and to provide a convenient ledge for plates. The range hood connects with the grill's exhaust to vent both cooking areas.

Lidia likes her Traulsen refrigerator because it has three separate compartments with individual thermostats so that meat, dairy, and vegetables stay at the appropriate temperatures. The Traulsen's ample ice drawer comes in handy for frequent entertaining.

As for small appliances, "I'm not too much into machinery except for my espresso machine and my big slicer," Lidia says. "The slicer is essential because we cure our own prosciutto and you need it for those thin slices of *affetate*, cold cuts. You must slice the prosciutto just before it's eaten, so you don't lose all the aromas." Lidia's favorite gadgets include a polenta cutter, open-weave pasta drying trays, and her *cripnia*, an Istrian cooking pot used to slow-cook meat and vegetables under the coals in the grill.

Lidia designed her home kitchen with distinct areas for cleanup and food preparation. She chose Chicago faucets and Elkay stainless-steel sinks because, she says, they hold up well under heavy use. On one side of the grill, the double vegetable sink is just a step away from the refrigerator. On the other, the cleanup area has a commercial Champion dishwasher with a 5-minute cycle that Lidia says is essential in a kitchen that feeds a lot of people. The cleanup sink features a built-in slanted drain board.

Even her art reflects Lidia's keen interest in everything culinary.

*Erminia and Giovanni, Erminia's beau, **right,** savor a two-pasta lunch. Though the dining table is closer to the tall windows overlooking Long Island Sound, panoramic water views reach to the working end of the kitchen as well.* ***Below,*** *Lidia uses portable cutting boards on her granite counters.* ***Opposite,*** *The Traulsen refrigerator has separate compartments for storing food at different temperatures. The big slicer is handy for cutting home-cured prosciutto.*

Past the cleanup area is a pantry whose long service counter extends to the dining room. The countertops provide plenty of room to fill dessert plates for more formal meals. Lidia calls her dining room "American style" and says she doesn't use it much because it "cuts the cook off from the party."

Although Lidia's kitchen has clean, modern lines, it also says Old World. Tiled walls, granite countertops, a terra-cotta floor, and custom cherry cabinets add to the look. The dish cabinets were modeled after her grandmother's old-fashioned freestanding cupboards, but Lidia's have etched glass doors above. "I told the architects I wanted the Italian feel—Italian surfaces and materials," Lidia says. "That's what Italian design does, it embraces the old, but puts it comfortably alongside the super-slick, modern thing. Think of a Ferrari parked in a piazza."

As a small child, Lidia spent a lot of time with her Grandmother Rosa, who taught her about selecting and processing food. This was her "first phase of learning cooking"—digging potatoes, drying peas and tomatoes, making vinegar, curing prosciutto, and kneading dough. Lidia laughs, "I still remember learning the dough with my hands—bread dough, gnocchi dough, pasta dough—they all feel different." She describes their diet as "primary food—we bought an animal and used everything." Later, her great aunt, who was a professional cook, taught her "the next level"—attention to presentation, how to compose an orchestrated meal of several courses, how to choose the best produce. She loved it all, and learned rapidly.

Now she carries on the teaching tradition with her granddaughter, Olivia, who as a toddler is learning to distinguish thyme, basil, and rosemary. "Kids record first and most easily with their olfactory sense. Their sense of taste is a tabula rasa, so you have to build it

up," Lidia explains. Joseph, Olivia's father and Lidia's son, is Lidia's key partner in the restaurant. Lidia's mother, who at 78 is still the center of the extended family, together with her beau, Giovanni, tend the vegetable garden that stretches across the front yard. Lidia also dries tomatoes and beans and cures prosciutto. When guests are expected, everyone pitches in to help roast a suckling pig on the big courtyard grill.

In addition to her busy home, Lidia juggles a wide array of food-related activities. She has two cookbooks, did a 26-part TV cooking show, and produces a line of sauces, "Lidia's Flavors of Italy." She also has a gastronomic travel company, which she runs with her daughter, Tanya. The 1998 opening of Lidia's in Kansas City came about because Lidia felt it was time to take her cuisine to the heart-

land. She goes there regularly to train cooks and make sure that her namesake restaurant maintains her vision.

Lidia predicts that long-cooking techniques like soup making will make a comeback. "All you need is fire and a pot. You have such wonderful mellowing and harmonizing of flavors, and you have a complete meal in a pot." In *Lidia's Italian Table* she explains the appeal of soup: "To come home and see the windows *appannate* (glazed with steam), to have the aroma of *pasta e fagioli* greet you at the door means you will soon be comforted from the inside out."

In 1994, Lidia flew to Croatia and planted an olive grove on her grandparents' land. She says the young trees are a symbol of peace, her gift to the war-ravaged area. During the fighting in the former Yugoslavia, Lidia organized shipments of food to her homeland. This Italian chef, mother, and grandmother shares her love of life and good food wherever she goes.

Above, The whole family tends the vegetable and herb gardens in the front yard.
Right, In a grapevine-covered courtyard outside the kitchen door, a large grill and pizza oven make it easy to prepare food for large groups. The grill is also a fine spot for air-drying the summer's last tomatoes and beans.

Lidia's granddaughter, Olivia, is learning to distinguish thyme, basil, and rosemary. "Kids record first and most easily with their olfactory sense," explains Lidia.

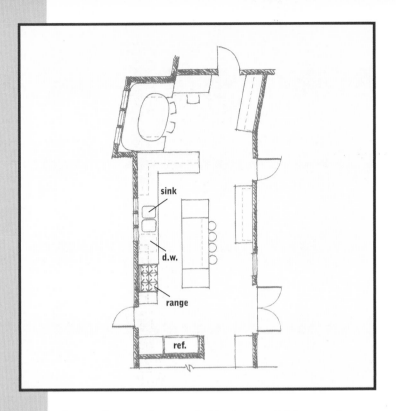

sink

d.w.

range

ref.

"We wanted a nice, clean kitchen. It's not 'gadgety' and it's very open to the outdoors. You open the windows. You open the doors. And you cook."

Joachim Splichal

Patina Pinot Restaurants

After leaving Germany, Joachim Splichal worked in top kitchens around the world before settling in Los Angeles. He and his wife, Christine, opened Patina, which Zagat's survey has named as L.A.'s favorite for eight years in a row. Other Splichal ventures include the five Pinot restaurants and cafés at three L.A.-area museums. Honored as Best California Chef by the James Beard Foundation in 1991, he wrote the Patina Cookbook—Spuds, Truffles and Wild Gnocchi.

Opposite, The twins demonstrate another use for the kitchen island.

For Joachim Splichal and his wife, Christine, 1996 was a very big year: They expanded their business beyond Los Angeles for the first time, adding restaurants in Pasadena and the Napa Valley to an already-substantial culinary juggernaut; bought a sprawling Mediterranean-style home with extensive gardens in San Marino; and, in an instant, doubled the size of their family with the arrival of twin boys.

*The extensive pantry, **left,** features floor-to-ceiling closets with storage for dried foods, equipment, and linens. **Below and opposite,** the kitchen's sleek island provides convenient work surfaces of granite and wood, as well as a good place to pull up a stool and eat breakfast or watch cooks in action. Narrow, glass-front drawers surround the island on three sides.*

Because there was so much going on in their lives, the couple hoped to move in to their new home and renovate later. Joachim remembers, "We didn't plan on doing much to it, but pretty soon we had to do everything because the plumbing broke down, the electricity was not sufficient, you name it." Although the house was substantial and gracious—with large rooms, tile roof, balconies, and meandering courtyards—little had been changed since it was built in 1919. Faced with major repairs in most of the house, Christine and Joachim decided to remodel their dark, outdated 30-year-old kitchen, too.

"We basically ripped everything out," Joachim says. "We wanted to create something that functioned very well as a kitchen but that also would be a comfortable, attractive living space. Most of all we wanted it to feel like a home—not a commercial kitchen." The plan called for compact, efficient work areas and lots of handsome maple cabinets for equipment storage. The couple also wanted easy access to the courtyard, a table for casual meals, and plenty of natural light and fresh air.

With those goals in mind, they decided on a domestic Wolf range, a KitchenAid Superba dishwasher, and a Kohler double-basin enamel sink, all installed in a row. Just a few feet away, Joachim placed his island with everything a chef, or home cook, could want. Next to large-paned, double French doors leading to the patio, a former hallway was opened up to create an ample dish and food pantry and a home for a second Sub-Zero refrigerator. At the other end of the kitchen, walls were taken down to create a cozy eating alcove, complete with wrap-around banquette. To satisfy the light and air requirements, existing windows were enlarged and a few new ones added. "We knew we wanted a nice, clean space," Joachim says. It's not 'gadgety' and it's very open to the outdoors. You open the windows. You open the doors. And you cook."

Both Christine and Joachim prefer a "put-away" look. "I don't like hanging pots and pans, or stuff sitting out on counters," he says. Not surprisingly, their kitchen amounts to a textbook on ingenious cabinetry and storage ideas. Joachim designed the center island and specified a myriad of features, including a dazzling bank of glass-front drawers for dry ingredients around three sides of the island. In the drawers, rich brown lentils, split green peas, pastas, Brittany sea salt, star anise, wild rice, red beans, and peppercorns make a colorful—and practical—display. Joachim says, "When you want some salt, you have it right there and you just grab it."

Joachim's island also boasts large maple chopping blocks at either end, a granite work surface in the middle, and both vertical and horizontal storage drawers—some very deep for large pots and pans. (Joachim favors WMF pans, made in Germany. "That's what my father used to cook with. They'll hold for 100 years.") Joachim especially wanted a good place for sitting on stools at the island, with room for knees underneath the generous overhang. "I like that because in the morning we eat breakfast at the island and when we have guests they can sit comfortably right in the kitchen and talk to us while we cook."

The built-in banquette also provides a pleasant place to sit. Its alcove is simultaneously an arty, 1950s statement—with bold fabrics

and hard-edged furniture—and a cozy, out-of-the-way spot for reading, eating, and conversation. Large windows flood the table with natural light, and after dark, a quieter, more intimate feel is produced by the stylized paper "spotlight." Along one wall, additional cabinets provide storage for delicate wine glasses above and for good china in roll-out drawers below.

The couple puzzled over how to separate the eating alcove from their busy kitchen, while keeping it integrated with the overall space. They asked their architect, Dan Nulty of Santa Barbara, to come up with some solutions, and eventually settled on a counter that juts out at right angles to the main work area, creating a natural alcove. Overhead cabinets with rippled glass doors on both sides let natural light shine through and provide the added benefit of access to the cabinets from either the kitchen or the eating area.

More interesting glass comes into play as backsplashes on walls around the sink. The frosted, light-green glass has beveled edges and adds a subtle touch of color. Christine got the idea from the kitchen in their old house.

Now that it's finished, Joachim and Christine can think of little they'd change about their kitchen, except that it should probably overtake the rest of the house. "I wouldn't have a separate living room or a dining room because we live in the kitchen," Joachim says. As if to prove that statement, the couple has begun to expand their cooking and eating space, first to the courtyard with an extensive barbecue, beautifully weathered paving stones from France, a dining table, and wrought-iron "candeliers." Next, on the other side of the courtyard, they are turning an old guest house into a stunning kitchen for entertaining (one entire side of the building opens to the pool). This second kitchen will be furnished European style, with an old oak farm table, lots of baskets, an antique German butcher block, a French bar from a bistro—complete with copper sink—and traditional baker's shelves. It will, perhaps, remind them both of their roots—

Opposite, The Splichals prefer a "put-away" look, so their kitchen is richly endowed with maple cabinetry. The cabinet shelves hold delicate wine glasses, and roll-out drawers below cradle dinner plates, cups, and serving pieces. *Left,* At home Joachim prepares simple meals with produce from local farmers. *Below,* He uses durable German-made WMF pots and pans, which spread heat evenly.

Christine's in Biarritz, where her parents ran a catering and pastry business, and Joachim's in Germany.

Joachim grew up in Spaichingen—a medium-sized village near Stuttgart—where his parents ran a *gasthaus.* Because their small inn served daily meals and his uncle's butcher shop was nearby, Joachim recalls being "always around food." Although young Joachim "wanted to go into management initially," he ended up in a kitchen in Holland. "Then I traveled and worked cooking—Israel, Norway, Sweden, Canada, Switzerland, Tunis, until I discovered Southern France."

After stints at La Bonne Auberge and L'Oasis, Joachim landed an apprenticeship with the great Jacques Maximin at Nice's Hotel Negresco. There he rose to the lofty sous-chef position. "It was very, very long hours, hard work, and though I was just a kid, I was the second in command. It was difficult to make some of the older cooks believe that I could run the kitchen when the chef was away. On top

The built-in banquette and 1950s furniture create a cozy, out-of-the-way nook that's flooded with natural light. After dark, the paper "spotlight" illuminates the alcove. Overhead cabinets with rippled glass doors define the eating area and let natural light filter through.

of it all, I was a 'dumb German,' so it wasn't easy. They thought I was too young and from the wrong country." But Joachim's uncompromising nature helped him stick it out for three years—in spite of occasional fist fights and crates of lobsters heaved at him.

Joachim came to Los Angeles in 1981 to work as executive chef at the Regency Club. A year later, he moved to the Seventh Street Bistro and also met Christine Mandion, who had left her native France

to study for a master's degree in international business—working for the family catering business was not what she wanted. "The first week I was here for school, I met Joachim and we began dating. So I get away from the food business and right away I fell in love with a chef," she says wryly.

The couple married in 1984 and opened Max au Triangle in Beverly Hills the same year. Although lauded by critics, the location was bad and the restaurant closed within months. In 1989, the Splichals opened Patina on Melrose Avenue, with Joachim running the kitchen and Christine handling the front of the house. Patina was profitable and enormously popular. The glowing reviews started rolling in. After sampling the chef's barley risotto, smoked beef tenderloin with horseradish-glazed potatoes, followed by *crème brûlée*,

Left, The island's multi-sized drawers—some extra deep for pots and pans—make convenient storage. In the pantry beyond, floor-to-ceiling closets house more equipment and food. *Below,* French doors to the courtyard let in plenty of light and air.

Ruth Reichl, *Los Angeles Times* food critic, wrote, "Food this good is a thrill to eat; it reminds you how glad you are to be alive."

Two short years after Patina was launched, Christine and Joachim went on to create "the Pinot Family" of restaurants, with the opening of Pinot Bistro. Now, the burgeoning "family" also includes Café Pinot, Pinot Blanc, Pinot Hollywood, and Pinot at the Chronicle. Restaurants at three L.A.-area museums and Patina Catering are also part of the Splichals' culinary empire.

Awards have been proliferating as well. For eight years in a row, Patina has been chosen by Zagat's survey as the top restaurant in Los Angeles. Joachim was named Best California Chef by the James Beard Foundation in 1991 and has twice been nominated for Chef of the Year by them. But the top-of-his-game chef quickly transforms into a smiling, soft-spoken daddy when the twins appear.

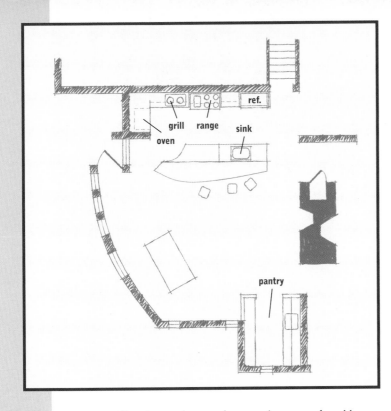

grill
oven
range
ref.
sink
pantry

"This is my spot. I stand and cook, and all my friends can fit in this kitchen...sit there or lean up against the counter and talk while I work."

Lydia Shire

Biba Pignoli

Lydia Shire owns two of Boston's favorite restaurants, Biba and Pignoli. She trained at London's Cordon Bleu and then came home to cook at Maison Robert before a stint at the Harvest Restaurant in Cambridge, Massachusetts. After helping Jasper White open Seasons at the Bostonian, she stayed on as executive chef for five years. In 1986, Lydia went west to open the Four Seasons Hotel in Beverly Hills. Two years later she launched Biba. The James Beard Foundation named her Best Chef in the Northeast in 1992.

Opposite, Lydia's kitchen merges her love of cooking with a keen artistic sensibility.

The first brush stroke of Lydia Shire's kitchen was a lipstick red Chambers stove from the 1930s. Although she spotted the stylized antique in Los Angeles and didn't even own a house at the time, she knew that, "if it was a red Chambers, it was mine." In essence, the stove was a metaphor that blended Lydia's two passions, art and cooking. Besides, red is her favorite color. So Lydia bought it, shipped it back to Boston, and stored it until she could find it a home.

*The cornerstone of Lydia's kitchen is a brilliant red 1930s Chambers stove, **above right.** Its stove-top broiler beats contemporary ranges for cooking lobster, fish, or thin cuts of meat, **above left.** The stove's oven is somewhat small, so Lydia added a state-of-the-art Gaggenau oven that's wide enough for the largest roasting pan. The stylish kitchen cabinets are made of sycamore and set off with stunning ebony trim, **left.***

In 1990, after establishing Biba, her award-winning Boston restaurant, Lydia and her husband, Uriel Pineda, bought a neglected Greek Revival house in the country. The house needed a total renovation, but Lydia saw it as a blank canvas on which to create her own work of art. Neither the "dreadful" staircase, which shot up just a few feet inside the front door, nor anything else inside the house was worth saving. But the land—part of a 60-acre plot that originally comprised an agriculture school—was a treasure, enhanced by the fact that much of the adjacent area is a Harvard University arboretum.

The couple gutted the house, retaining only the shell and front door. Heading up the project was Lydia's daughter, architect Lisa Shire, who transformed a maze of tiny rooms into an ample, gracious kitchen with plenty of space for casual entertaining. "This is my spot right here," says Lydia. "I just stand and cook, and all my friends can fit in this kitchen. People like to sit there or lean up against the counter and talk while I work." In addition to space for entertaining, Lydia wanted a relatively compact, clean-looking kitchen that would work for large-scale cooking.

To supplement the Chambers, Lydia chose two extra-large Gaggenau burners that accommodate oversize pots and pans. "I don't need gadgets, but, boy, do I need room to cook. I always make too

Designed by Lydia and her daughter, architect Lisa Shire, the dish pantry provides a completely functional space as well as a highly decorative kitchen element. The see-through walls of the pantry are fashioned of a shimmer-ing metallic grid sandwiched between two plates of glass. The shelves display a rich and varied collection of antique and modern serving pieces, teapots, Magnalite roasters, and copper cook-ware. Although the dish-washer in the pantry is a backup for the unit in the kitchen proper, it's invaluable during the holidays and after parties.

Lydia doesn't like things to match, so she uses an eclectic mix of antique and "foundling" chairs around her 16th-century Dutch tavern table, **above.** A wall with glass sidelights was designed to hold Lydia's treasured French poster of a woman holding a fish. The hand-blown, red glass chandelier is from Murano, an island outside Venice known for its fine art glass. **Right,** Lydia debated the flooring material for months, but after seeing a floor she liked in a Seattle restaurant, she quickly decided on polished concrete: It's attractive, easy to maintain, and much more affordable than the other materials she considered.

much food—there's no such thing as 'just enough' in my house. My luxury is to have those two big burners." Lydia also invested in a Gaggenau oven, which is wider than the Chambers' oven, and a Fry-o-lator, because she and her husband, a native of Colombia, like to make empanadas.

But the Chambers is the mainstay. Lydia loves it because it's easy to maintain and provides an eye-catching centerpiece for the heart of her home. It also has unique features that are missing from modern stoves, such as a warming container (perfect for mashed potatoes) and a stove-top broiler that is raised and lowered with a lever.

"It's good for haddock," Lydia says. "I leave the skin on the haddock. And then I make some nice little garlic crumbs for the top and I put the fish here and lower the broiler. Delicious. My son, Alex, loves fish cooked that way." The oven in the Chambers also has superior qualities. "There's something about the heat from these old-fashioned ovens—it puts a little crust on the cake or cookies that I love. It's almost as if the modern ovens have heat that's too even."

Lydia installed her sink and cleanup area across from the cooking areas. At just under 4 ft. from one counter to the other, the space isn't too narrow, but still just a step across. The deep 35-in. by 18-in.

Above left, Lydia's cook-in fireplace has a multi-speed rotisserie that produces perfect spit-roasted meats for parties and holidays. The fireplace is constructed of the same local fieldstone that is used for the walls and patio just outside the kitchen door. *Above right,* Lydia collects all kinds of whimsical art, including these accurately scaled culinary miniatures. *Right,* Lydia's eating counter is a work of art in itself. Fashioned of polished concrete, with insets of copper and mirrors, the counter provides a good place for friends and family to perch and talk to the chef while she works.

Lydia's impressive display of glasses of many shapes and high-styled dining table accessories are from all over the world. She especially enjoys Italian glass and loves intense colors.

apron sink and counters are fashioned of dramatic Ubatuba granite, which is greenish black with flecks of gray and green. The sink's extra-large drain empties quickly. "A large drain for an oversize sink is smart," says Lydia. The high, arching Herbeau faucet (a French brand) turns off gently but firmly and accommodates large pots. The kitchen has no garbage disposal because the septic system can't handle it, but Lydia doesn't miss it. Under the counter is one of her favorite kitchen features—a large, hidden garbage can. "I hate those little tiny things that you fill up in two seconds."

Lydia set the counter height at 38 in. because she dislikes working at low counters. "See, right here I can stand perfectly straight and do my thing," she says, chopping an onion. "After working in professional kitchens you learn that it makes such a difference if your counters are high enough so that you don't have to bend your back." On the opposite side of the working counter is a polished cast concrete eating counter by artist Tom O'Connell. It boasts whimsical touches: little stairs cut into one side, bits of polished copper, mirrors, and art-glass insets.

Lydia stores small appliances in an appliance garage, "because I want things to look clean." She doesn't own a microwave. "When I make tea, I surely don't mind boiling a pot of water, and we use frozen foods so seldom that I wouldn't have need for a microwave. This kitchen doesn't have a lot of gadgets, and I like it that way."

Large appliances are another matter. Lydia favors Traulsen refrigerators. She has two—one in the kitchen and a second in an outdoor shed. She likes the door and drawer configuration and the quality of ice the Traulsens produce. "I'm kind of fussy about ice," she admits. "This ice is beautiful. It tastes great."

Two ASKO dishwashers also are essential. One is under the sink and the other is tucked in the dish pantry. "I think auxiliary appliances can make a positive difference in how well a kitchen functions." Lydia doesn't use the pantry dishwasher often, "But I'll tell you, when it's Thanksgiving or we have big parties, it's so handy."

Although the dishwasher is central to the pantry's design, it is barely noticeable because there's so much else there. Lydia's pantry is like a jewel box. The see-through walls, made of a metallic grid between two pieces of glass, shimmer while softly revealing what's inside: art-glass serving pieces, antique platters, and Magnalite roasters and casseroles.

Lydia and her daughter designed the sleek, modern sycamore cabinets. She added ebony trim to emphasize the different-size cabinet doors, because Lydia prefers things that don't match perfectly. Mark Ritchie, who did the woodwork at Pignoli, Lydia's second restaurant, built the cabinets in her home kitchen.

Lydia comes by her artistic and culinary abilities naturally. Both of her parents were well-respected fashion illustrators, and her father was a great cook. "When I was about four, I started chopping garlic and doing other tasks for him in the kitchen." Although she wanted to go to art school, she wasn't accepted at her first choice. Instead, Lydia fell in love, got married, and had three children right away. When her marriage ended, she enrolled at the Cordon Bleu in London. Back in Boston, her resume included Maison Robert, the Harvest Restaurant, the Copley Plaza, and the Parker House. But her culinary

After the kitchen remodel, Lydia mounted a television on the wall just above the fireplace so that she can watch her beloved New England Patriots play football on Sundays while she cooks a big dinner.

creations at the Seasons restaurant at the Bostonian Hotel brought the opportunity for Lydia to open the Four Seasons in Los Angeles.

When she opened Biba, the restaurant was heralded almost as much for its bold decor as for its novel food, which includes foie gras on buckwheat Indian paper bread and tangine of chicken and yams. The *Christian Science Monitor* described Biba as an expression of Lydia's friendly, generous nature and of her love for peasant foods, vibrant flavors, and casual gatherings.

Warm, red accents suffuse Lydia's home kitchen, from a delicate Murano glass chandelier to the red painted floor-to-ceiling steel win-

dows that stretch along the curving back wall of the house. Made by the Hopes Company in Pennsylvania, these windows are like those used in schools all across America in the early 1900s. Lydia found their proportions appealing; her daughter came up with the idea to do them in bright red. It was also Lisa's idea to use a gradation of wider panes to accentuate the wall's pleasing curve.

Most of the kitchen's design was purposeful and exact. Other aspects evolved as the project took shape. "It's interesting how some things happen—like the polished concrete floor. That was basically a product of running out of money, but I love it." She first considered a number of different stones, but with such a large area to cover, the floor would have pushed them over budget. Then Lydia visited a

Left and above, *Floor-to-ceiling, red steel–framed windows form a gently curving wall along the back of the house and effectively fuse the wooded, rolling countryside and kitchen. Usable outside space is added by the fieldstone patio just through the kitchen door. For formal dinners, Lydia loves her dining room, complete with its own collection of charmingly mismatched chairs, Italian burlwood table, tile-accented fireplace, and hand-painted, bronze-colored ceiling,* **opposite.**

Seattle restaurant that had a polished concrete floor. "When I came back, I said 'Yes, we have to do a concrete floor.' The price was less than half of the other materials."

A few details had to be changed after the kitchen renovation was finished. Extra lighting was installed over the 16th-century Dutch tavern table so that Lydia and Uriel can read there or play cards at night. The wall-mounted television was added so Lydia can watch her beloved New England Patriots while she cooks Sunday dinner.

Lydia serves food directly on the Italian dining table because she likes the way the wood looks. Although the table has acquired a few burn marks from errant candles, Lydia says, "You know in the end, I really don't care. It's like my philosophy of chipped plates. Little knocks and dings show that things are used and loved."

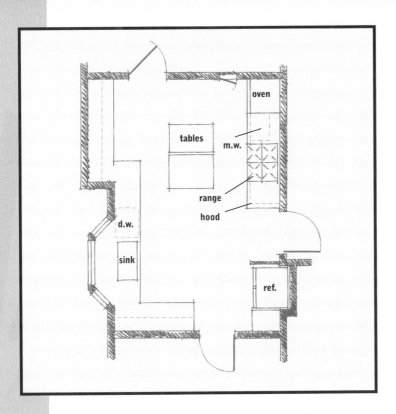

LaBrea Bakery
Campanile

Mark Peel and Nancy Silverton own Campanile and LaBrea Bakery in Los Angeles. Mark trained at top restaurants, including Spago; Nancy graduated from the Cordon Bleu and Le-Notre pastry school and worked at Michael's and Spago. In 1990, Nancy won the James Beard award for Best Pastry Chef. Mark has been nominated three times by the Beard Foundation as Best California Chef. Recent books include Nancy Silverton's Breads from the LaBrea Bakery *and* Food of Campanile.*

Opposite, *Two great chefs share one great kitchen.*

"You can have a professional kitchen at home. But that's not what we wanted here...."

Mark Peel Nancy Silverton

Team up two of America's top chefs, and the whole is greater than the sum of its parts. With Mark Peel guiding Campanile—one of L.A.'s premier restaurants—and Nancy Silverton at the helm of LaBrea Bakery next door, lucky Los Angeleños get a complete dining experience: from Mark's grilled prime rib with black olive tapenade to Nancy's hand-crafted breads and heavenly desserts.

Above, Nancy collects culinary treasures—especially those of interest to a pastry chef. Antique chocolate molds perch on an oak plate rail in the dining room. **Right,** She replaced the solid wood doors of the upper cabinets with bubble-patterned wire glass, for an antique look. Lower cabinets were painted dark brown, yellow, and cream, and have vintage, unpolished brass pulls. Work surfaces run around three sides of the kitchen. **Opposite,** The sink's bay window makes a sunny, protected place for Nancy's display of antique whisks, beaters, and choppers.

The collaboration on the renovation of their kitchen wasn't always as seamless, they say, but the result is a kitchen that Nancy and Mark feel perfectly suits their house and the size of their family.

Mark and Nancy bought their 1919 Craftsman-style home five years ago. It had the appeal of being within five minutes of Campanile and LaBrea, had plenty of room for their three children—Vanessa, now 16, Ben, 13, and Oliver, 4½—and offered a welcome change from their kitchenless apartment over the restaurant and bakery.

Previous owners had modernized the ample, rectangular kitchen by installing unpainted wood cabinets with shiny hardware, bright white tile countertops, and new oak floors. "When we moved in, I thought the kitchen space and layout were really workable, but the cabinets were new oak, which I hated, and we needed to replace the appliances," Nancy recalls. To give the kitchen a look more in harmony with the character of the 80-year-old house, Nancy and Mark decided to use paint, ingenuity, and just a few major purchases, rather than a full-blown remodel. "We just worked with it, including keeping the placement of the appliances the same. If it had been a tiny kitchen with no counter space we would have ripped everything out and started over, but that wasn't necessary here."

Left, Craftsman-style tiling in soft, subtle colors was designed by Lori Erenberg to provide a vintage, unifying look for the kitchen. Wheat-motif tiles behind the cooktop are Nancy's favorites. Another collection—odd, humorous, old-fashioned food tins—sits on the cooktop hood. Mark chose the Dacor cooktop for its good BTU output and slim profile; he can still use the drawers underneath to store knives. **Opposite,** The dining room and "homey" kitchen connect well.

They began by replacing the front panels of the upper cabinets with bubble-patterned wire glass. With dark brown, yellow, and cream paint on the remaining woodwork and vintage, unpolished brass drawer pulls, the cabinets acquired the requisite old-fashioned look. The wooden farm tables in the center of the room add to the quaint atmosphere. They make a good chopping or mixing surface as well as a comfortable place to pull up a stool and eat breakfast.

Craftsman-style tile in subtle gray-greens, chocolate brown, and ochre replaced the bland white tile installed in the '70s. Nancy and Mark asked designer Lori Erenberg of Los Angeles to make the new tile "look like it had always been there." Inspiration came from the intricately tiled living room fireplace, the couple's favorite dishes, and Nancy's profession: The golden-brown, wheat-motif tiles used behind the cooktop are indeed apt for this world-class baker's kitchen. So the countertops would be easier to wipe clean, Nancy and Mark specified thin grout lines in the food preparation areas.

While tiling and cabinet work progressed, Mark began his search for high-performance, domestic appliances that would fit in the existing spaces. He feels that for residential use most people don't need professional-level equipment, unless they routinely cook for a large number of people. Mark chose a four-burner Dacor cooktop because it has good BTU output, is simple to clean, and it fit. Its thin top-to-bottom profile allowed Nancy and Mark to retain the drawers underneath the cooktop, where Mark likes to store his favorite knives by Constant, a German manufacturer. He selected two KitchenAid ovens, convection and regular, because they are durable and fit the space. When it came to the KitchenAid refrigerator, though, Mark says it was a different story. "We had to shave the cabinet's wood edge a little to squeeze the new fridge in and we took a bite out of the closet behind." He chose a Bosch dishwasher because "it's quiet, saves on water, and does a good job."

Nancy and Mark opted not to replace the existing porcelain trough sink because it's large and deep enough for big pots, and because its location in a sunny alcove makes a pleasant spot to wash dishes. Perhaps more important, the alcove creates an out-of-the-way niche for Nancy to display some of her culinary collectibles. "I have my little collections of antique whisks and beaters and choppers. I like to look at them. I don't want them put away in closets or drawers. They're colorful and add personality to the kitchen." It's a good thing that behind-the-sink space was available because Mark likes "utilitarian kitchens. I don't like a lot of junk on the counters. The best design thing most people can do is to get rid of all the nonessential stuff sitting out."

Nancy and Mark met in 1979 at the popular Michael's restaurant in Santa Monica, where both worked. Nancy had returned from studies at the Cordon Bleu in London when she heard the buzz about Michael's—*the* place for up-and-coming cooks to prove themselves. She was hired as cashier, the only job available at Michael's, but vowed to work her way up to the kitchen. Before long an opening came up as assistant pastry chef. Nancy says, "It still wasn't what I wanted to do, but it was a little closer to a burner and farther away from the computer" cash register. Although she had never done pastries and says she was intimidated by the rigidity of pastry classes at

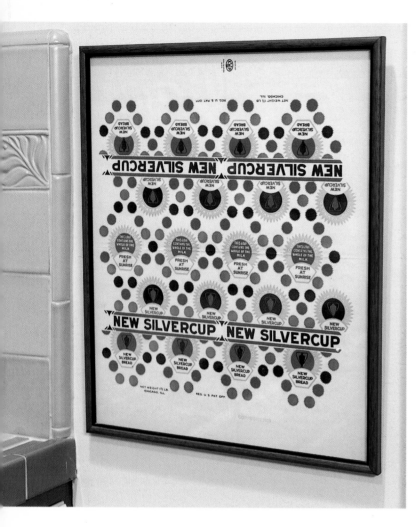

a half hour to make dinner for three kids, so she had a limited repertoire. I do remember helping cook the yams with marshmallows on top for Thanksgiving dinner—that was a lot of fun. In high school, I found a job at a little dinner place. In retrospect, I think the food wasn't great, but it was certainly a lot better than anything I'd seen before." There, Mark learned enough basic kitchen skills to keep him employed part-time while attending college.

He also discovered that he wanted to cook for a living, so he transferred to the Hotel and Restaurant Management School at California Polytechnic University in Pomona. Mark quickly landed a part-time job as prep cook, "turning" vegetables at Wolfgang Puck's small but influential Ma Maison. Other influences on Mark's budding career were work in agricultural economics at the University of California at Davis and a European tour of apprenticeships at three-star restaurants. On his return, he worked at Ma Maison again and at Chez Panisse. Then Mark was tapped to be chef at Puck's newest venture, Spago. During their search for Spago's pastry chef, Mark recommended Nancy, and the two soon were working together again.

the Cordon Bleu, Michael's pastry chef showed her there was room for creativity and flexibility in a personal approach to dessert making. "I ended up loving it," she says. She even went back to the famed Le-Notre school in France to fine-tune her pastry skills.

Both Nancy and Mark say their passion for cooking came not from early exposure or inspiration, but from simply doing it. Nancy remembers working in her college cafeteria. "One day I was chopping or whisking and I thought, 'I love this. This is what I want to do when I grow up.'" Once Nancy decided she wanted to cook, she tenaciously pursued her chosen craft; for a while she even worked for free at 464 Magnolia—a small, chef-owned restaurant in northern California—because, as she puts it, "I found it all so very exciting."

Mark seemed to just fall into cooking, too. "My mother was a single, working mom. She'd come home from teaching and have about

The couple stayed at Spago for 3½ years, married, and then moved to New York. Soon they decided that California would be the location for their first joint enterprise because of the availability of fine, seasonal produce. Their plans for a Tuscany-inspired restaurant with a bakery next door were galvanized by their travels in Italy—where they were captivated by the simple cuisine based on perfect, ripe ingredients—and by Nancy's love of baking bread and creating down-home desserts.

Opposite left, Nancy's collection of bread wrappers is from the 1920s and '30s, when sliced bread first became available. She loves the colorful designs. *Opposite right,* Craftsman tiles in food preparation areas have extra-thin grout lines for easy cleaning. *Above,* Nancy whisks up an omelet, using eggs just gathered from the Auracana hens in the backyard.

They opened LaBrea Bakery first, in January of 1989, after renovating a down-at-the-heels building with imitation Moorish tower and perfecting a modest list of breads—country white, olive, rye, walnut, and a baguette. Campanile was launched five months later and immediately garnered rave reviews, both for its stunning architecture of lofty glass roofs and tower—reincarnated as an Italian campanile—and Mark's menu of bright, intensely flavored dishes such as swordfish grilled on rosemary branches and warm poached mozzarella in tomato basil broth. Nancy's rustic breads and creative pastries such as ricotta cheesecake with pine nut brittle are an integral part of the Campanile experience. The two halves of the enterprise have been phenomenally successful; Campanile is a perpetual top draw in Los Angeles, and LaBrea Bakery turns out enough bread to supply hundreds of retail outlets. The restaurant-cum-bakery concept has been widely copied.

Working together so closely can sometimes be difficult for Nancy and Mark, but having their comfortable house and renovated, cozy kitchen nearby (not overhead) makes a world of difference. Nancy underscores the point: "You can be a professional restaurateur and choose to have a professional kitchen at home. But that's not what we wanted here, because we really just cook meals for our family, and we like to entertain with simple meals shared among friends. We don't do 'show-off' cooking at home."

Both advise keeping it simple. Nancy says, "Just give me my mortar and pestle. I use it every day to grind garlic or make a creamy mayonnaise dressing." Mark agrees. "It's good to have a few spoons,

Opposite, Two antique farm tables form a work island. When Nancy and Mark moved into the house, they ripped up the kitchen's new oak flooring because they thought it didn't look right with the dining room's old oak. Underneath they found Douglas fir floors, which they decided were perfect. **Left,** Mark adds a little spice. **Below,** Oliver likes to help dad collect the backyard eggs.

whisks, and spatulas out in a convenient place. I think that's much better than having a lot of fancy machines." Nancy does no baking at home, except to make cookies with the kids—the only time she uses her KitchenAid mixer. She muses, "I always think that when I retire a freestanding mixer will come in handy." Mark's ears perk up: "When you're retired," he says, "you're going to bake more chocolate chip cookies?"

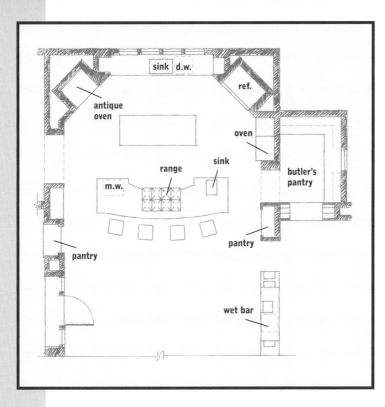

Lafitte's Landing

Lafitte's Landing at Bittersweet Plantation is John Folse's award-winning Cajun/Creole restaurant in Donaldsonville, Louisiana. John hosts a PBS television series, A Taste of Louisiana, *and talk radio's* Stirrin' It Up. *White Oak Plantation, his catering and special-events facility, is in Baton Rouge. Louisiana Premier Products produces John's prepared foods for restaurants, food-service, and retail establishments. John's once-a-year promotional restaurants have introduced the world to Cajun/Creole cuisine. He has written seven cookbooks.*

Opposite, *Pouring it on.*

"I didn't want to say, 'This is the kitchen, here's the family room.' It's all one…. When you come to my home, you come to my kitchen."

John Folse

"A lot of delicious dishes, like crawfish étouffé and venison jambalaya, originated in the hunting camps of Louisiana," says Cajun chef John Folse. "Great hunters, fishermen—and cooks!—came out of my culture, mostly because of the wild country, the swamplands. In the old days, families would camp out on the nearest bayou for a few days," he explains. "Then, everybody'd pitch in to make these lip-smacking one-pot meals out of everything they'd shot, trapped, picked, or pulled up on a line."

While John's splendid new kitchen might seem a long way from a primitive hunting camp, it's designed so he can get back to his roots in an instant.

John and his wife, Laulie, began planning their new house several years ago. Although they loved living at "Bittersweet"—a graceful, 1853 Acadian plantation home that had been in Laulie's family for generations—the Folses wanted to build their own place. They decided to build in Gonzales, on the historic River Road, which follows the Mississippi's curves from Baton Rouge to New Orleans. There they could remain close to John's acclaimed restaurant, Lafitte's Landing, and live not far from where he grew up on Cabanocey Plantation.

John is quick to point out that his family was "land poor." The plantation had been prosperous under his great grandfather, Victorin Zeringue, but the family fortune was diluted by an abundance of heirs and by agricultural changes. John talks of his early years in a "Cajun shack," one of eight children whose mother died early. In spite of privations, though, love and good cooking were always at the heart of the Folse's family life.

Opposite, At one end of the kitchen/great room, John has an impressive array of modern equipment, as well as an antique stove. Floors are wax-rubbed, tongue-and-groove Louisiana pine. *Above,* A massive brick fireplace commands the other end of the great room, with a painting of Papa Noël hanging over the hearth. *Left,* Archways lead to the butler's pantry and dining area.

In laying out his own home, John resolved that the kitchen would be its center. "I decided that I wanted to build a kitchen in a great room, and then just add whatever else we needed to it. I didn't want to say, 'Okay, this is the kitchen, here's the family room, and the living room's through there,'" John says. "It's all one... .When you come to my home, you come to my kitchen."

In addition, John wanted an "old French look," professional-grade home appliances, and suitable areas to display—and use—his antique cooking equipment. John and Laulie also thought it important to blend indigenous, historic building materials into the plan.

Working with Baton Rouge architect Henry Carville, the couple came up with a kitchen and great room that fulfills all their wishes. The main, 21-ft. by 65-ft. space features 2-ft.-thick walls, banks of gracefully arched doorways, soaring ceilings with mortise-and-tenon beams, and floors made from centuries-old Louisiana pine. The massive, freestanding brick chimney with plantation kitchen fireplace provides cooking-over-the-coals at one end of the room; John's modern kitchen stands at the other.

While busy at his centrally located cooktop, John can survey the room, visit with friends lounging by the fire, or look outside "to see my vegetables growing." Down one long side of the room, doorways open to the outdoors and to the sunny, cypress-paneled breakfast room. Archways opposite lead to the butler's pantry and dining area.

John's kitchen features cabinets made of Louisiana cypress—originally used to build plantations in the 1700s and tracked down through a lumber broker. T&L Forest Products of Baton Rouge fashioned the cabinets with flush doors and traditional beadwork.

The massive center work table is also made of antique cypress, with a maple butcher block top and English cast-iron drawer pulls. "I had a picture of a beautiful old table from a butcher's shop, so we decided to re-create it exactly, except we inset mahogany strips between the maple boards." The table has open shelves at each end with contents in full view; "I like to look at these things because each one has a story—every dish, every bowl, every platter."

The cast-iron pot rack decorated with crowing cocks was a lucky find from a Louisiana antique store. John collects rooster-motif kitchen objects, so he was delighted when he ran across the rack, which now displays antique and new English copper pots. John prefers his old cast-iron pots and pans, however. "Every pot that's made in the world today is made to mimic the qualities of cast iron. And none of them ever cooked better than these pots I inherited from my Uncle Paul."

John designed a brick-lined niche for his late-1800s American Enterprise stove. The unusual piece is the cornerstone of John's collection of historic ranges (others are on display at his office). One oven and the broiler run on gas while the bottom oven is wood-fired. After several years of painstaking restoration, the range now keeps perfect temperature and looks as beautiful as the day it was made.

For all his major modern appliances, John decided to go with Viking. He explains, "I wanted all my equipment to be handsome, functional, and easy to use." The two wall-mounted, 36-in.-wide thermal convection ovens, the refrigerator/freezer, dishwasher, and warming drawer all are "Graphite Gray"—a dark gray, matte finish. Of the ovens, John says, "The settings are so simple. You hit the temperature and set it. Then, when it reaches the right heat, it beeps real nice for y'all."

Above left, John uses antique open-hearth cooking implements. His late-1700s "hastener" has a clock-wound rotisserie that turns meat for 30 seconds in one direction, then reverses. A tray below holds vegetables. *Above right,* The butler's pantry stores three generations of plantation china. Two-foot-thick walls contain wine racks. *Left,* The pantry window features a rooster and a carp, symbols of the kitchen from the Eastern and Western Hemispheres.

The six-burner cooktop sits in the expansive island, with a second sink close at hand. A pop-up downdraft vent was necessary, because it would have been nearly impossible to vent the cooktop up to the barn-height ceiling.

The garbage disposals are Viking, too. John recommends a disposal in every kitchen sink—and oversize, 6-in.-diameter drain pipes. "You're always throwing something down there that you shouldn't, you know?" He also went with larger gas lines (1½ in.) and 1-in. copper water lines, for power, pressure, and flexibility.

The brass and copper light fixture over the cooktop was designed to look like one from an old Mississippi River paddleboat. Below the fixture, the island's dark Ubatuba granite reflects light and nicely sets off the wood in the room.

A 220-volt outlet by the cooktop accommodates John's cappuccino maker. Plenty of outlets are stationed around the kitchen, "so I don't have to run around with an electric knife or a blender trying to find a place to plug it in," the chef says.

The great room floors are wax-rubbed, 1½-in.-thick tongue-and-groove Louisiana pine. John and Laulie proceeded cautiously with the new floor's color—adding one drop of stain at a time "until the knots started to come out dark and the gold started to really show nicely and the grain just picked up." Flooring in the butler's pantry and dining area is easy-care ceramic tile that resembles slate.

The butler's pantry stores precious china, large soup tureens, platters, and heirloom table linens. A deep drawer has interior racks designed for hanging delicate tablecloths. The upper cabinets have glass shelves, so the light shines through. "There's three generations of plantation china in here," John says. "I want to be able to see it."

John and Laulie's breakfast room, opposite the butler's pantry, has floor-to-ceiling windows that open to the cook's garden. "That's all the food pantry I need," John states—though he actually has two small pantry closets for dry goods. "The fresh herbs are all there and plenty

The six-burner island cooktop may be John's command post, but Laulie likes to lend a hand. Rooster motif art and equipment are favorites of John's. The cast-iron pot rack with crowing cocks was a lucky find from a local antique shop. John had the hanging light fixture made to look like one from a Mississippi paddleboat. An open archway leads to the breakfast area, where spacious windows look out to John's gardens—his fresh "pantry," where all the plants are edible varieties.

of fruit trees, sassafras trees—for filé powder—and a couple of grape arbors. When I was designing this kitchen, I didn't want a pantry with all kinds of canned goods," John says. "Fresh is best."

This quick harvesting of what's at hand is linked to what John charmingly calls "the swamp floor pantry," a cornerstone of Cajun cooking. "The Cajuns"—French Canadians exiled from Nova Scotia in 1755—"ended up in South Louisiana with nothing more than their black iron cooking pots," he says. "Their cooking style reflects ingenuity and survival. They gathered and used all the ingredients they could get their hands on."

For one-pot cooking, John enjoys using his beautiful brick fireplace and antique open-hearth cooking implements. John's culinary antiques include a late-1700s "hastener" with a clock-wound rotisserie, a quail roaster, and a French, wrought-iron crane with an ivy motif. "According to tradition, when a house was new, the owners would have all their friends over to hang the crane in the fireplace together. There's even a Longfellow poem about it," Laulie explains.

John's own family traditions center on cooking. "I was fortunate to have been reared in a family of good cooks," he says. Mary Ferchard, who cooked for the family after John's mother died, "really knew how to harvest the wild greens and bring out all the real flavors of Louisiana." John's father also had an influence. "He domesticated us fairly early," John explains, "by making sure that we knew how to make a roux and a good gumbo."

Howard Johnson's restaurant was the unlikely location of John's first professional kitchen experience. The budding manager trainee didn't like washing dishes at first, "but soon it started to make sense that to really run a restaurant you should know how to do everything." John stayed with the chain for three years, moving up through its ranks. In 1973 he was hired to be chef of the Prince Murat hotel in Baton Rouge, where he came under the tutelage of Chef Fritz Blumberg.

Finally, after 10 years of honing his cuisine of native Cajun flavors with a classic French overlay, John was asked by a local bank to salvage "The Tavern" restaurant in downtown Baton Rouge. He did such a good job that he was named a co-owner, and soon took on another restaurant of his own—Lafitte's Landing in Donaldsonville.

Set in a 1797 Acadian-style mansion on the river, Lafitte's was not an instant success. John says, "If I'd known anything at all about the business, I'd never have opened Lafitte's way out there." One day, though, he was following a plantation tour bus down the road and said to himself, "That's my market right there, on the hoof." He called

all the tour companies and made arrangements for scheduled stops at Lafitte's. Soon he had 10 or 15 buses each day pulling in for lunch. Next, John turned his attention to high-end customers, and Lafitte's became a romantic, special-occasion "destination" restaurant halfway between Louisiana's two largest cities.

In 1985, John decided to take his cuisine to other countries. With several-week stints in such cities as Hong Kong, Paris, Bogota, and Moscow, he introduced locals to the "taste of Louisiana."

Later, having succeeded with a multi-season PBS cooking show, syndicated radio show, seven cookbooks, a catering operation at White Oak plantation, and a food products company with more than 100 offerings, John remained irrepressibly enthusiastic.

Then came a bump in the road. In October 1998, shortly after celebrating its 20-year anniversary, Lafitte's Landing burned. After weeks of heartache and confusion, scrambling to come through for their pre-fire holiday bookings and comforting their loyal staff, John and Laulie made the decision to re-open in the all-too-aptly named Bittersweet Plantation. Within several months of the fire, Lafitte's was again serving such delicous Cajun/Creole dishes as velouté of crawfish, corn, and potatoes and black-eyed-pea battered shrimp.

At home, John appreciates "having access to all the different cooking methods—firing up the wood oven, broiling squash, making ham with kumquat glaze in a black iron pot, or roasting a chicken in my hastener." He demonstrates, "I baked these cat-head biscuits in the wood oven this morning. All you need for those biscuits is a steady 375° and a big bowl of melted butter to dip 'em in," John grins. "It's all great fun."

Favorite Home

The Best Sautéed Crab Cakes

HUBERT KELLER

Fleur de Lys

Serves: 4

3½ oz. sea scallops
1 whole egg
salt and freshly ground pepper
½ c. cream or half-and-half
1 lb. fresh jumbo lump crab meat
1 Tbsp. finely chopped cilantro
2 Tbsp. peeled, seeded, and diced tomato
1 tsp. Dijon mustard
3 drops Tabasco sauce
1 Tbsp. olive oil

Place the sea scallops and the egg in a blender. Process with about 5 on-and-off pulses. Add a dash of salt and freshly ground pepper. Mix together well. With the blender running, slowly pour the cream (or half-and-half) through the feed tube. Season to taste.

Thoroughly chill the scallop mixture and the remaining ingredients before mixing.

Spoon the sea scallop mixture into a mixing bowl. Add the crab meat, having removed any bits of shell and broken up any lumps. Add the chopped cilantro, diced tomato, Dijon mustard, Tabasco, salt, and pepper. Mix together delicately and check the seasoning.

Shape the crab mixture into 8 patties (about ¾ in. thick and 2½ in. across) and refrigerate for 15 minutes.

To cook, heat the olive oil in a large, heavy sauté pan, arrange the crab cakes in the pan, and brown them lightly, 2½ minutes on each side.

Serving suggestion: Season baby lettuces with an olive oil or walnut oil vinaigrette and place the leaves in the center of each plate. Garnish the side of the plate with cooked asparagus tips. Top the lettuces with the crab cakes. Decorate with slices of toasted baguette bread and a Tbsp. of diced tomato. Serve the remaining vinaigrette on the side.

Used with permission from *The Cuisine of Hubert Keller* (Ten Speed Press, 1996).

Diver Sea Scallops with a Fennel Salad & Orange Olive Oil Emulsion

TERRANCE BRENNAN

Picholine

Serves: 4

Dressing
3 c. fresh orange juice, strained
½ c. + 1 oz. extra virgin olive oil
sea salt and pepper to taste
2 Tbsp. fresh chopped cilantro
1 med. fennel bulb
½ red bell pepper
½ yellow bell pepper
½ small red onion

12 pc. large sea scallops, cleaned
¼ c. kalamata olives, pitted and halved
1 bunch arugula, cleaned

Put the orange juice in a non-reactive pot and reduce to 1 c. Let cool to room temperature. With a hand blender, emulsify with ½ c. olive oil. Add salt and pepper to taste and cilantro.

Take the core out of the fennel, keeping it whole. Slice paper thin on a slicer or mandolin. Trim the ends off the peppers and clean out the seeds and white piths while keeping the peppers whole. Slice as per fennel. Peel and clean the red onion and slice half as per peppers and fennel. Reserve the other half for another use.

Season the sea scallops to taste with salt and pepper. Add 1 oz. olive oil to a 12-in. non-stick sauté pan. Over medium heat, sauté the scallops for approximately 1 minute on each side.

Put the fennel, arugula, peppers, onions and olives in a bowl. Toss with 4 oz. of the orange dressing. Place the salad in middle of 4 plates. Place the scallops around the salad and pour 2 oz. of the dressing on top and around the scallops. Serve immediately.

Eggplant à la Szechwan

CECILIA CHIANG

Betelnut

Serves: 2-4

5 Chinese eggplant (the long banana-shaped variety)
2 Tbsp. coarsely ground pork
3 c. cooking oil
2 coarsely minced scallions for garnish

Seasoning #1
3 cloves garlic, minced
1 tsp. minced fresh gingerroot
2 Tbsp. Chinese rice wine (sherry can be substituted, if rice wine is unavailable)

Seasoning #2
2 Tbsp. hot bean paste
2 Tbsp. chicken stock
1 Tbsp. white vinegar
1 Tbsp. chile pepper oil
1 tsp. sugar

Seasoning #3
1 tsp. toasted sesame oil

Trim off the stems of the eggplant. Quarter the eggplant lengthwise and cut into 3-in. slices. Mince ingredients as necessary for *Seasonings #1 and #2*.

Heat the cooking oil in a wok until very hot and braise the eggplant for 1 minute. Remove the eggplant from the wok and drain it in a strainer.

Remove all but 1 Tbsp. of oil from the wok and add *Seasoning #1*. Introduce the minced pork and brown it for a minute. Add the eggplant to the wok and stir-fry for 30 seconds. Add *Seasoning #2* and continue stir-frying for another 2 minutes to reduce the ingredients into a sauce.

Add *Seasoning #3* and stir-fry for another 30 seconds. Remove from the wok. Sprinkle the garnish on top of the dish and serve.

Recipes

Lamb Tikka

MARK MILLER

Coyote Café & Red Sage

Serves: 8-10

1 qt. plain yogurt
½ peeled white onion
2 whole garlic cloves, peeled
2 bunches cilantro, leaves only
2 jalapeños
1 Tbsp. peeled grated fresh ginger
⅛ tsp. saffron dissolved in ¼ c. hot water
1 tsp. ground black pepper
1 tsp. salt
½ tsp. ground cumin
¼ tsp. ground cardamom
1 Tbsp. paprika
2 Tbsp. vegetable oil
1 whole boned leg of lamb with all
    the outside fat trimmed off (approx.
    4-5 lb.), tied up with butcher twine

Put all the ingredients except the lamb into a large blender and purée until smooth. Put the lamb in a ceramic or stainless-steel bowl, pour the marinade over the lamb and rub all over, cover with plastic wrap, and refrigerate for at least 12 to 24 hours. Turn the lamb in the marinade every couple of hours.

Take the lamb out of the refrigerator at least 4 hours before cooking, still turning it in the marinade. Place the lamb on a rotisserie spit over indirect heat over the grill or in the fireplace. Cook for approximately 2 hours, basting constantly with marinade, until internal temperature is about 135°F. Take the lamb off the spit and let it rest for 10 minutes. Carve into thick slices.

Serve with basmati rice and other Indian vegetables or lentils.

Aïoli Provencal

ALICE WATERS

Chez Panisse & Café Fanny

Serves: 6-8

1 sm. head garlic
½ tsp. coarse salt
1 egg yolk
2 c. of the best French olive oil

Peel the garlic (about 12 cloves). When choosing the garlic, make sure it has small, juicy cloves and hasn't started germinating. Later in the year, if you cannot find garlic without a green sprouting germ, be sure to cut each clove in two and remove the germ: it is bitter and hard to digest. Chop the garlic coarsely, put it in a mortar with the salt, and work to an even paste. Add the egg yolk and build up very slowly with oil as you would for a classic mayonnaise, using the pestle or a wooden spatula. If you are a purist, you can skip the egg yolk, or replace it with some breadcrumbs soaked in water and squeezed dry. This will give you a strong aïoli, better eaten for lunch and followed by a long siesta.

Serve with salt cod (soaked in the refrigerator for 24 hours in three or four changes of water and simmered until soft in unsalted water flavored with thyme, bay leaves, black peppercorns, and garlic); boiled potatoes and carrots; hard-cooked eggs; and cooked snails, all served together in a large dish, with the aïoli in its mortar.

Used with permission from *Chez Panisse Vegetables* (HarperCollins, 1996).

Chicken, Oyster & Andouille Gumbo

JOHN FOLSE

Lafitte's Landing

Serves: 6

1 c. vegetable oil
1¼ c. flour
2 c. diced onions
2 c. diced celery
1 c. diced bell pepper
¼ c. minced garlic
1 large baking chicken, cut into serving
    pieces
1 lb. sliced andouille
3 qt. chicken stock
1 pint oysters; reserve liquid
2 c. sliced scallions
1 c. chopped parsley
salt to taste
cracked black pepper to taste
Louisiana Gold Pepper Sauce to taste

In a 2-gallon stockpot, heat the oil over medium-high heat. When hot, add the flour, and using a wire whisk, stir constantly until a dark brown roux is achieved. Do not scorch. If black specks appear, discard and begin again. Add the onions, celery, bell pepper, and garlic. Sauté 3 to 5 minutes, or until the vegetables are wilted. Add the chicken and andouille, blending well into the vegetable mixture. Add the chicken stock and oyster liquid, one ladle at a time, blending well after each addition. Bring to a rolling boil, reduce to a simmer, and cook approximately 2 hours or until the chicken is tender. When tender, add the oysters and cook 5 minutes more. Add the scallions and parsley and season to taste with salt, pepper, and Louisiana Gold Pepper Sauce. Serve over steamed white rice.

Note: Usually ⅛ tsp. of filé powder (ground sassafras leaves) is sprinkled on top of the plated gumbo for that perfect Louisiana finish.

Brick-Roasted Chicken with Asparagus and Chanterelle Mushrooms

CHARLES DALE
Renaissance

Serves: 4

2 whole chickens, approximately 3 lb. each
2 fireproof bricks, 2-3 lb. each, wrapped in aluminum foil
2 Tbsp. chopped fresh sage
1 Tbsp. fresh orange zest
2 cloves garlic, chopped
¼ tsp. ground chipotle chile, or ⅛ tsp. cayenne
1 tsp. ground cumin
½ c. olive oil
1 orange, not peeled, sliced into 8 rounds

Sauce:
½ c. fresh orange juice (or substitute concentrate)
½ c. dry sherry (or substitute vermouth)
4 c. chicken stock
2 Tbsp. olive oil
1½ lb. fresh chanterelle mushrooms (or substitute portobello or domestic), washed and sliced
2 bunches fresh asparagus spears, sliced diagonally ¼ in. wide by 2 in. long

Remove the first and second joints from the chicken wings and set aside. Stand the chicken upright, and cut down the length of the backbone on either side. Remove the backbone and set aside. Lay the chicken flat and cut down the center of the breastbone. You should have 2 chicken halves. Repeat with the remaining chicken.

Make the marinade by mixing the chopped sage, orange zest, garlic, chipotle, ground cumin, and olive oil together. Liberally coat all the chicken halves with the marinade, and stack them in a covered plastic container, alternating each layer with the orange slices. Refrigerate for 2 to 3 hours.

Meanwhile, roast the chicken backs and wings in a roasting pan in a 400° F oven until golden brown. While these are roasting, reduce the orange juice in a 2-quart saucepan until syrupy in consistency. Immediately add the sherry or vermouth, and cook for 5 minutes. Add the chicken stock, and bring to a boil. Add the roasted chicken backs and wings, and lower to a simmer. Cook for 1 hour, strain, and reserve the sauce.

Heat two 12-in. ovenproof skillets on the stovetop over high heat. Add 1 Tbsp. of olive oil to each one, and add 2 chicken halves to each pan, skin side down, to sear chicken. Cover each pair of chickens with one brick, and place in the oven. Roast at 400° F for 20 minutes, then remove the bricks, and turn the chickens over so the skin side is up. Roast for another 20 minutes, remove the chickens from the pans, and allow to rest for 5 minutes in a warm place.

Meanwhile, divide the chanterelles and toss them into the hot pans. Sauté for 2 minutes, stirring, and then add the sauce. When the sauce boils, add the asparagus slices, cook for 2 minutes, and add salt if necessary.

Spoon the mushrooms and asparagus onto individual plates (or into a serving dish), place one chicken half on top of each plate, and spoon the sauce over each one. Serve immediately.

Crispy Vegetable Stir-Fry

KEN HOM
Imperial City

Serves: 4

4 oz. red bell peppers
4 oz. green bell peppers
4 oz. yellow bell peppers
4 oz. fresh or canned (drained weight) water chestnuts
2 oz. canned (drained weight) bamboo shoots
2 tsp. oil, preferably groundnut
2 tsp. salt
3 slices fresh ginger
2 oz. snow peas, trimmed
3 Tbsp. water

Cut the peppers into 1½-in. triangles. Thinly slice the water chestnuts and bamboo shoots.

Heat the oil in a wok or large frying pan. When it is moderately hot, add the salt and fresh ginger. Stir-fry for about a minute to allow the ginger to flavor the oil. Add the peppers and stir-fry for 2 minutes. Then add the water chestnuts and bamboo shoots and continue to stir-fry for 2 minutes. Finally add the snow peas. Stir-fry for 30 seconds and then add the water. Stir-fry for another minute or until the snow peas are cooked, adding more water if necessary. When the vegetables are thoroughly cooked, turn them onto a platter and serve at once.

Sake-Cured Hot-Smoked Salmon with Japanese Pickles

TOM DOUGLAS
Dahlia Lounge & Etta's Seafood

Yields: 8 small appetizer servings

Marinade:
1 c. soy sauce
¾ c. brown sugar, packed
½ c. water
¼ c. sake
8 coins sliced ginger, ⅛ in. thick
1 Tbsp. chopped garlic, or 6 cloves
2 tsp. kosher salt

1 lb. salmon fillet, cut into 1- to 2-oz. pieces
nonstick spray
8 sage leaves
Japanese Pickles (see below)

Whisk the marinade ingredients together until the sugar dissolves. Put the salmon pieces in a non-reactive container and pour the marinade over the salmon. Allow to marinate overnight. Remove the salmon from the marinade (saving a little to brush over the top just before smoking), place the pieces on a rack sprayed with nonstick spray set over a baking sheet and let sit, refrigerated, 2 hours to allow the glaze to set. Place a sage leaf on top of each piece of salmon, and brush each one with marinade. In a smoker, cold-smoke for 25 minutes, and then hot-smoke at 325°F until cooked, about 15 minutes.

Japanese Pickles:
1 English cucumber, cut in half and sliced on the bias ⅛ in. thick. (You don't need to peel and seed an English cucumber, but if you substitute a regular cucumber you should peel and seed it.)
¾ c. rice wine vinegar
¼ c. water
3 Tbsp. sugar
4 tsp. kosher salt
2 tsp. peeled and grated ginger

Place the sliced cucumbers in a heatproof container. In a small saucepan on medium-high heat, combine the vinegar, water, sugar, salt, and ginger. Bring the mixture to a boil, stirring to dissolve the sugar. Pour the hot liquid over the cucumbers. Allow to "pickle" for ½ hour or longer. Serve as a garnish for sake-cured smoked salmon or on other Asian dishes or bento.

Roast Chicken
NORA POUILLON
Restaurant Nora & Asia Nora

Serves: 4

4-5 cloves garlic, peeled and thinly sliced
2 Tbsp. olive oil
½ tsp. salt
½ tsp. freshly ground black pepper
2 lg. sprigs tarragon
one 3- to 4-lb. large roasting chicken

Heat the oven to 350°F.

Toss the thinly sliced garlic with olive oil, salt and pepper.

Loosen the skin from the chicken breast and slide the seasoned garlic slices and a sprig of tarragon under the skin on each side.

Truss the chicken.

Rub the skin with the remaining seasoned oil, lay the chicken on its right side in a roasting pan and cook for 20 minutes.

Turn the chicken onto its left side (at each turn, baste the chicken with the juices in the pan), cook for an additional 20 minutes, and then turn the chicken onto its back to finish roasting for last 20 minutes.

Cut into serving portions.

Grilled Monkfish Brochette with Bacon and Garden Herb Butter
JEAN PIERRE MOULLÉ
Chez Panisse

Serves: 4

2 med. angler fish tails (monkfish)
Fleur de Sel and black pepper
1 Tbsp. olive oil
¼ c. dry white wine (Chateau Bonnet)
chives, parsley, and chervil, minced
*   (reserve parsley and chervil stems)*
4 slices smoked bacon, ½ in. thick
¼ lb. sweet butter (surgeres or echiree)
2 shallots, diced

Clean the fish by removing the gray skin and taking off the center bone. Portion into 2-in. cubes, and season lightly with Fleur de Sel and black pepper. Drizzle with olive oil and a splash of white wine, and marinate for 10 minutes with the stems of the parsley, chervil, and a few chives. Slice the bacon into small lardons and spear alternate pieces of fish and bacon on bamboo skewers (3 to 4 pieces of fish are sufficient for lunch).

Prepare the compound butter with the diced shallots and the minced herbs. Season with Fleur de Sel and pepper.

Prepare the grill. I prefer to use vine cuttings for the flavor or you can use mesquite charcoal. When ready, place the brochettes on the grill and cook for 8 to 10 minutes on each side.

In a warm platter, spoon half of the butter, arrange the brochettes on it and add the remaining butter on the fish. Let sit for a few minutes so the flavors combine.

Serve with a garden salad for lunch or boiled potatoes for dinner.

Bow-Tie Pasta with Asparagus and Shrimp Sauce
LIDIA MATTICCHIO BASTIANICH
Felidia & Lidia's

Serves: 4

1 lb. asparagus
5 Tbsp. olive oil
2 cloves garlic, minced
½ lb. sm. shrimp, peeled, deveined and
*   cut in half*
salt and hot pepper flakes to taste
1 lb. bow-tie pasta
10 leaves fresh basil, shredded
2 Tbsp. Italian parsley, chopped
2 Tbsp. grated Parmigiano Reggiano
*   cheese*

Cut off bottoms of asparagus. With a potato peeler, pare outer tough skin, cut in 1 in. pieces, and steam.

In a pan, heat the olive oil, sauté the garlic until golden, add the shrimp, and sauté for 3 minutes. Add the asparagus and seasoning.

Boil the pasta. When done, drain and reserve ½ c. water.

Add the drained pasta to the sauce, add the reserved water, basil, and parsley. Stir over a flame for a few minutes, remove, add the Parmigiano Reggiano, stir, and serve immediately.

Grilled Lobster
LYDIA SHIRE
Biba & Pignoli

Serves: 2

2 live 1½- to 1¾-lb. lobsters

For the tomalley collected from the 2 lobsters:
3 Tbsp. softened butter
2 Tbsp. chopped fresh parsley
1 clove garlic, finely minced
2 tsp. fresh breadcrumbs
½ stick butter, melted to brush on cut
*   lobster to broil*

Drawn butter:
1 stick unsalted butter, melted
¼ tsp. salt
black pepper
lemon

Preheat the broiler.

Split the live lobsters in half. Remove the sac (brain) behind the eyes and discard. Remove the tomalley (green liver) and reserve.

In a small bowl mix the tomalley (the green liver) with the softened butter, parsley, garlic, and crumbs.

Brush the cut side of the lobster with melted butter and place close to the broiler heat. Broil 3 minutes or until you start to see a little golden color on the tail meat. Immediately divide the tomalley mixture equally into the four cavities of the lobster. Return to the broiler. Broil an additional 3 to 5 minutes, or until the tips of the large claws have turned black. This is a foolproof method to know the lobster is cooked.

The lobster is ready to eat. You won't need much if any of a sauce to dip the lobster in—the buttery tomalley acts as that.

Should you want some drawn butter on the side, melt good-quality unsalted butter. Add salt, a few grinds of black pepper, and a good squeeze of lemon.

Pot Roasted Guinea Hen
FRANK McCLELLAND
L'Espalier

Serves: 4

2 Guinea hens, 2½ lb. each

Marinade
3 shallots, minced
3 cloves garlic, minced
½ c. white wine
zest of 1 orange
¼ c. olive oil
Juice of 2 oranges
1 Tbsp. coarse prepared mustard
8 juniper berries, crushed
2 tsp. dried sage
1 tsp. dried thyme leaves
1 tsp. dried tarragon leaves
3 bay leaves, crushed

To prepare the dish
Peanut or grapeseed oil
1 c. Madeira
2 c. white wine
1 c. chicken stock
4 cloves garlic, unpeeled
12 fingerling potatoes, unpeeled
12 baby carrots
6 baby fennel bulbs, split in half
    lengthwise
12 pearl onions, peeled and blanched
1 bunch fresh sage leaves, reserve some
    for garnish
1 bunch fresh tarragon leaves, reserve
    some for garnish
salt and pepper to taste

With a sharp knife, cut the backbone out of the hens. Remove the leg and thigh in 1 piece; leave the breast on the bone.

Combine all the ingredients for the marinade and pour over the hens. Let marinate 5-6 hours, or overnight.

Remove the hens from the marinade. Season with salt and pepper.

Heat the oven to 400°F.

Heat a large skillet over medium-high heat. Add just enough peanut or grapeseed oil to coat the pan with a thin film. Brown the hens about 3 minutes on each side, until evenly colored.

Remove the hens from the pan and place in a deep, covered baking dish. Pour any oil out of the skillet and add the Madeira and white wine. Bring to a boil while scraping any of the browned bits off the bottom of the pan. Cook for 1 minute. Pour over the hens. Add the remaining ingredients to the baking dish and cover tightly. Bake for 25 minutes.

Remove the hens from the broth, place on a cutting board, and cover with foil while you finish the dish. Strain the vegetables from the broth and divide among 4 serving plates. Skim any excess oil from the broth and place on stove, bring to a boil, and reduce by half.

When the broth has reduced, cut the breast off the bone and cut the leg and thigh pieces in two.

Arrange the pieces of hen on each serving plate. Check the broth for seasoning and ladle some on top of each portion. Garnish with additional fresh herbs if desired and serve immediately.

Wild Mushrooms Cooked in the Coals
PAUL BERTOLLI
Oliveto

Serves: 4

4 large handfuls of mushrooms (I like to
    use meaty wild mushrooms such as
    chanterelles and porcini for this recipe;
    use 1 handful per serving)
salt and freshly ground pepper
good extra-virgin olive oil
lemon

Wash and trim any dirt away from the mushrooms and cut them into thick chunks. Season with salt, pepper, olive oil, and a squeeze of lemon.

To form a large package with baking parchment: Cut a large rectangle and fold it in half. Open the parchment and lay the mushrooms onto one half. Bring the top over and crimp the edges tightly. Now envelop the packet in a similar fashion using heavy-duty aluminum foil.

Form a bed of ash about 2 in. thick on the hearth below or to the side of the fire. Place a layer of embers evenly over the ash, then cover the embers with another 1 in. of ash. Place the mushrooms in the fireplace for 30 minutes.

Alternatively, bake the mushrooms in a similar manner in a moderately hot oven.

Remove the parchment from the foil, place it on a platter and open it at the table.

Cauliflower Soup with Shaved Black Truffles
ANNE QUATRANO AND CLIFFORD HARRISON
Bacchanalia & Floataway Café

Yields: 8-10 cups

Chicken stock
2 whole chickens, rinsed
2 tsp. kosher salt
2 ribs celery, cut in 2-in. pieces
2 carrots, cut in 2-in. pieces
1 whole head garlic, cut in half crosswise
1 Spanish onion, quartered
1 bay leaf
stems of thyme
stems of parsley

2 heads cauliflower, removed from stem
    and cut into florets
2 qt. chicken stock (recipe above)
½ c. heavy cream
2 Tbsp. unsalted butter
salt and pepper to taste
¼ tsp. freshly grated nutmeg
truffle oil (optional)
1 black truffle (optional)

Place the chickens in an 8-qt. stockpot, and fill with cold water to cover. Add the salt and place over high heat. As soon as the liquid comes to a boil, reduce heat to a simmer and skim off the foam on top. Add all the vegetables, bay leaf, and herb stems, and simmer on low for 3-4 hours. Strain through fine sieve. Reserve the chicken meat for soup or salads. Allow the stock to cool overnight in the refrigerator. Skim the fat off the top and reduce the stock by one-quarter. It is now ready to use or freeze for later.

Bring 2 qt. of chicken stock to a boil and add the cauliflower. Bring back to a boil and then reduce the heat to a simmer. Cook until the cauliflower is tender and cooked. Purée in a food processor or with a wand processor. The consistency should be smooth and silky. Blend in the cream and butter. Season with salt, pepper, and nutmeg. Garnish with a drizzle of black truffle oil and a shave of black truffle.

Blueberry Pancakes

ANTHONY AMBROSE

Ambrosia on Huntington

Yields: Sixteen 6-in. pancakes

3 c. whole milk
2 c. buttermilk
¼ oz. dry yeast
⅓ c. maple syrup
1 Tbsp. sesame oil (can substitute with
    any nut oil)

Dry ingredients

4 c. all-purpose flour
½ c. sugar
2 tsp. salt
1 tsp. baking powder
2 tsp. baking soda

4 eggs, whites only
¼ lb. (1 stick) butter
1 pint blueberries, rinsed (can substitute
    fresh frozen)
vegetable spray, such as Pam

In a small saucepan, warm the whole milk and buttermilk over low heat approximately 3 minutes.

In a medium-size bowl, combine the yeast, maple syrup, and oil. Once the milk has warmed, add to yeast mixture and allow the yeast to activate. The mixture will become foamy when complete, approximately 15 minutes.

Meanwhile, sift all the dry ingredients in a large mixing bowl and set aside.

In a separate bowl, whisk the egg whites to peaks and set aside.

In a small saucepan, heat the butter over moderate to high heat until it browns. Remove from the heat.

Once the yeast has activated, fold the yeast mixture and browned butter in with dry ingredients, creating a batter.

Fold half of the egg whites into the batter, followed by the remaining half.

Over moderate heat, warm your flat skillet with vegetable spray, spoon 6 in. of batter onto warm skillet. Sprinkle with blueberries. When batter begins to bubble spray with vegetable spray and flip pancake. Pancakes will be dark and, due to the maple syrup, slightly caramelized.

Poached Fillet of Beef with Béarnaise Sauce

GEORGES PERRIER

Le Bec-Fin & Brasserie Perrier

Serves: 4

Broth

2 onions, peeled and studded with
    4 whole cloves, cut in half
4 center-cut beef shin bones, cut 2 in.
    thick
2 leeks (white part only), washed and
    coarsely chopped
1 bunch fresh Italian parsley
Bouquet garni (1 sprig fresh thyme, 2 bay
    leaves, 1 tsp. crushed peppercorns)

Vegetables and beef fillet

salt and white pepper
4 carrots, peeled
4 turnips, peeled
4 Idaho potatoes, peeled
1 bunch scallions (white part only)
1½ lb. center-cut beef fillet (completely
    trimmed of all fat and silverskin)

Béarnaise sauce

1 lb. (2 c.) clarified butter
1 Tbsp. dry white wine
1 Tbsp. chopped fresh tarragon leaves
2 lg. shallots, finely chopped
1 Tbsp. finely chopped fresh Italian
    parsley
¼ tsp. crushed black peppercorns
2 Tbsp. red-wine vinegar
4 egg yolks
2 Tbsp. water
salt

Cooking the broth: Prepare the broth at least 1 day before serving. Heat the oven to 400°F.

Heat a cast-iron or steel skillet until smoking hot, then place the onions cut-side down in the skillet and sear until dark brown. Remove from heat.

In a roasting pan, brown the beef bones in the oven for about 1 hour, or until well and evenly browned.

Place the beef shins and any browned bits from the pan, the onions, leeks, parsley, and bouquet garni in a stockpot. Cover with 4 in. of cold water and bring to a boil. Skim once and then reduce the heat to a simmer. Cook the broth for 4 hours, skimming occasionally. Strain through a fine sieve. Discard the vegetable solids. Remove the marrow bones from the beef shins and set aside. Cool the pot of broth in an ice bath and refrigerate overnight. The next day, remove and discard any solidi-

fied white fat on top of the broth. (The broth may be made up to 4 days ahead of time.)

Poaching the vegetables and beef: Bring the broth to a boil, reduce the heat to a simmer and season with salt and pepper to taste. Prepare the carrots, turnips, and potatoes by cutting them into tourné (seven-sided barrel shapes). Trim off the tops and bottoms of the vegetables, then cut into 1-in.-diameter rough oblong shapes. Using a sharp paring knife, cut each oblong into a seven-sided cylinder. Cook the carrots, turnips, and potatoes for 5 minutes in the simmering broth. Add the scallions and cook for 5 minutes more. Remove the vegetables from the broth and set aside.

Tie a cotton string around the circumference of the fillet. (This will keep its shape and make the cooking even.) Lower it into the broth and simmer for about 20 to 25 minutes, or until medium-rare (140°F on a meat thermometer). Remove the beef from the broth, cut off the string, and let rest for 5 minutes.

Making the béarnaise sauce: Warm the clarified butter. Place the white wine, tarragon, shallots, parsley, crushed pepper, and vinegar in a small stainless-steel or enamel pot and cook until almost all the liquid is evaporated. Transfer to the top of a double boiler, along with the egg yolks and water. Whisk constantly over boiling water until the eggs are thickened and fluffy. Remove the pot from the heat and, while continuing to whisk, slowly drizzle in the warm clarified butter. Season to taste with salt and keep warm.

Serving the beef: If you like, serve the broth as a separate first course. For the main course, slice the fillet into ¼-in.-thick rounds and then arrange in 4 shallow soup bowls with the vegetables and top each with 1 bone marrow. Moisten with a little of the cooking broth. Serve the béarnaise sauce on the side.

Used with permission from *Georges Perrier Le Bec-Fin Recipes* (Running Press, 1997).

Manila Clam Chowder

MICHAEL McCARTY
Michael's

Serves: 6

2 Tbsp. unsalted butter
1 med. Maui, Walla Walla, Vidalia, or sweet
 red onion, chopped
2 med. carrots, 1 chopped, 1 peeled and
 cut into ¼-in. dice
4 fresh white mushrooms, chopped
1 bunch parsley stems
salt
1 c. dry white wine
2 lb. Manila clams, scrubbed and rinsed
3 strips, each ¼ in. thick, smoked slab
 bacon, as lean as possible
1 med. boiling potato, peeled and cut into
 ¼-in. dice
1 med. zucchini, cut into ¼ in. dice
8 c. heavy cream
freshly ground white pepper
1½ tsp. chopped fresh chives

In a large pot, melt the butter over low heat. Add the chopped onion, chopped carrot, mushrooms, and parsley, sprinkle lightly with salt, and sauté, stirring occasionally, until the vegetables are soft but not yet browned, about 10 minutes.

Add the wine and raise the heat. When the wine boils, add the clams and cover the pot. Steam, shaking the pot frequently, until all the clams have opened, 3 to 5 minutes.

Line a sieve with a double thickness of cheesecloth and set it over a large bowl. Pour the contents of the pot into the sieve. Rinse out the pot and return the strained cooking liquid to it. Bring it back to a boil and boil it briskly until it has reduced by three quarters, 15 to 20 minutes.

Meanwhile, remove and reserve the clam meat from the opened clams. Discard any unopened clams along with the shells and cooked vegetables.

On a heated grill or in a skillet over medium heat, cook the bacon until crisp, about 2 minutes per side. Drain on paper towels. Cut the bacon crosswise into thin julienne strips and set them aside.

Bring a large pan of lightly salted water to a boil. Add the diced carrot and potato and cook until just done, about 2 minutes; then add the diced zucchini and cook for about 1 minute more. Drain.

Add the cream to the reduced cooking liquid and simmer briskly until the liquid is thick and has reduced by a third, about 15 minutes.

Add the reserved clam meat, vegetables, and bacon; simmer briefly to heat them through. Season to taste with salt and pepper, then ladle into heated soup plates and garnish with chives.

Used with permission from *Michael's Cookbook* (Macmillan Publishing Co., 1989).

Granola

PATRICK O'CONNELL
The Inn at Little Washington

Yields: 12 cups

5 c. rolled oats
1½ c. raw, unsalted cashews or cashew
 pieces
1½ c. untoasted shredded coconut
1 c. untoasted wheat germ
1 c. sesame seeds
1 c. soy flour
1 c. slivered almonds
1 c. safflower or other vegetable oil (not
 olive oil)
1 c. honey
nonstick spray

Heat the oven to 325°F.

In a large mixing bowl, combine all the dry ingredients using a wooden spoon. Add the vegetable oil and stir well. Add the honey and stir to combine.

Spray several large baking pans or cookie sheets with nonstick spray and spread the granola evenly about 1 in. deep in the pans.

Bake, turning frequently, for approximately 25 minutes or until golden brown. (If you prefer your granola in smaller pieces, it can be easily broken up while still warm.)

Let cool to room temperature and store in a large tin or in plastic bags. The granola will keep very well for several weeks or longer unrefrigerated.

Used with permission from *The Inn at Little Washington Cookbook: A Consuming Passion* (Random House, 1996).

Potato, Fennel, and Garlic Frittata

MARK PEEL AND NANCY SILVERTON
LaBrea Bakery & Campanile

Serves: 4

1 med. fennel bulb
6 eggs
1 tsp. chopped fresh tarragon or ½ tsp.
 dried tarragon
1 clove garlic, minced
¼ tsp. coarsely ground black pepper
3 Tbsp. olive oil
1 med. red potato, peeled and cut into
 1-in. cubes
6 lg. cloves garlic, sliced into thirds
¾ tsp. coarse salt
1 Tbsp. unsalted butter
3 to 4 oz. Jarlsberg or Swiss cheese, cut
 into ½-in. by 3-in. strips

Remove the top feathery greens from the fennel bulb, chopping enough to equal 1 Tbsp. and reserving the remainder whole.

In a medium bowl, whisk together the eggs, chopped fennel greens, tarragon, minced garlic, and pepper. Set aside, covered, for 1 hour or refrigerate overnight.

Remove any tough outer stalks from the fennel and cut the bulb horizontally into ¼-in. slices. In a 9- or 10-in. ovenproof skillet, heat 2 Tbsp. of the olive oil and sauté the potatoes and sliced fennel over moderate heat until tender, about 10 minutes. Transfer to a plate. Add the sliced garlic and sauté briefly. Return the vegetables to the skillet with the garlic, sprinkle with the salt, and toss together for 1 minute. Transfer all the vegetables to a plate and wipe the skillet clean with a paper towel.

In a skillet, melt the butter with the remaining 1 Tbsp. olive oil and add the egg mixture. Do not stir the eggs. Cook over low heat for 1 to 2 minutes, or until the edges begin to set, then spread the vegetables over the top. Arrange the cheese strips like spokes of a wheel over the vegetables, place under the broiler, and broil just until the cheese melts.

Carefully slide the frittata onto a serving plate, cheese side up. Garnish with reserved fennel greens.

Used with permission from *Mark Peel and Nancy Silverton at Home: Two Chefs Cook for Family and Friends* (Warner Books, 1995).

Chicken Quesadillas with Avocado and Cilantro Salsa

JOACHIM SPLICHAL
Patina & Pinot

Serves: 4

Salsa
2 tsp. extra-virgin olive oil
¼ sm. red onion, cut into ¼-in. dice
3 plum tomatoes, peeled, seeded, and cut into ¼-in. slices
1 Tbsp. tomato juice
½ sm. jalapeño pepper, seeded and minced (about 1 tsp.)
1 sm. clove garlic, very finely chopped
pinch of cayenne pepper
dash of Tabasco
1 Tbsp. finely chopped cilantro
juice of ½ lemon
½ avocado, cut into ¼-in. dice
salt and freshly ground white pepper to taste

Quesadillas
1 pasilla or Anaheim chile pepper
½ lb. chicken thighs
3 lg. flour tortillas
¾ c. grated Monterey Jack cheese
4 plum tomatoes, peeled and thinly sliced
2 Tbsp. finely chopped cilantro

In a small skillet, heat the oil over medium heat. Add the onion and sauté for 2 to 3 minutes, or until translucent. Remove from the heat and allow to cool for 5 minutes. In a medium mixing bowl, combine the remaining salsa ingredients and toss gently together until evenly mixed. Cover and refrigerate until ready to serve.

Heat a grill or broiler to high heat. Grill the chile pepper, turning, until evenly charred, then place it in a brown paper bag and seal the bag. When the pepper is cool enough to handle, peel, seed, and cut it into 4 equal squares. At the same time, grill the chicken thighs, turning to brown them evenly, until they are done through with no trace of pink remaining, 8 to 12 minutes. When they are cool enough to handle, slice the meat thinly and set it aside, discarding the bones.

Using a 3-in. cookie cutter, cut each tortilla into three 3-in. disks. You should have 9 equal disks (you will only use 8—the 9th is a chef's perk).

Assemble four 3-in. open ring molds on a tray that will fit into your refrigerator and place one of the tortilla disks in the bottom of each mold. Divide the quesadilla ingredients among the molds, layering them as follows: a little grated cheese, sliced tomato, chicken, pepper square, chopped cilantro and a little more cheese. Cover each mold with another tortilla disk and press down gently but firmly to compact the layers. Refrigerate the quesadillas for 2 or 3 hours to help them firm up before you finish the dish.

Finishing
¼ c. corn oil
cayenne
reserved salsa
4 sprigs cilantro

To finish, in a large nonstick skillet, heat 1 Tbsp. of the oil over medium heat. Remove the ring mold from the layered quesadillas, holding the top down with 2 fingers as you lift the mold up and away. Then, using a flat-ended spatula, transfer the quesadillas 2 at a time to the skillet and sauté until they are just barely golden and the cheese has melted, about 1 minute on each side. Press down gently on the top before turning each one so that the cheese will adhere to the tortilla and the quesadilla will hold together. Add another 1 Tbsp. of the oil before cooking the next 2 quesadillas, if necessary. Transfer the cooked quesadillas to 4 heated appetizer plates, sprinkle a little cayenne around the rim of the plate, and serve immediately, topped with a spoonful of salsa and a sprig of cilantro.

Used with permission from *Joachim Splichal's Patina Cookbook: Spuds, Truffles and Wild Gnocci* (HarperCollins, 1995).

Rustic Ranch-Style Soup with Tomato, Jalapeño, and Avocado

RICK BAYLESS
Frontera Grill & Topolobampo

Serves: 6-8

3 qt. rich chicken broth
1 lg. head garlic, unpeeled
1 lg. sprig fresh epazote (optional)
2 fresh jalapeño chiles, stemmed
1 med. white onion, cut into ¼-in. dice
2 lg. ripe tomatoes, cored, seeded, and cut into ¼-in. dice
salt, about 1½ tsp. depending on the saltiness of the broth
¾ c. loosely packed chopped cilantro
about 1 c. coarsely shredded cooked chicken (optional)
2 ripe avocados, peeled, pitted and cut into ½-in. dice
1 lime, cut into 6 to 8 wedges

The broth: Measure the broth into a large (6-qt.) pot. Slice the unpeeled head of garlic in half widthwise and add both halves to the broth along with the optional *epazote*. Bring to a boil, then simmer over medium-low heat, partially covered, for about an hour. The liquid should have reduced to about 7 c. Remove the garlic and *epazote* and discard.

Finishing the soup: While the broth is simmering, cut the chiles in half lengthwise and cut out the seed pod. Slice into very thin lengthwise strips and set aside with the diced onion and tomatoes.

Generously season the broth with salt, then add the chiles and onion, partially cover, and simmer for 7 minutes. Add the tomatoes, cilantro, and optional chicken and simmer another 3 minutes, then ladle into warm bowls. Garnish with the diced avocados, serve to your guests, and pass the lime separately for each to squeeze in to their liking.

Note: Add shreds of chicken to make it a main dish or squash blossoms for a dressy starter. Make this soup when you can get ripe tomatoes. Broth made from a good chicken will shine here.

Used with permission from *Rick Bayless's Mexican Kitchen: Capturing the Vibrant Flavors of a World-Class Cuisine* (Scribner, 1996).

Mexican Style Charcoal Grilled Chicken with Poblano Chile Rajas

ROBERT DEL GRANDE
Café Annie & Café Express

Serves: 2-4

1 whole chicken, cut into quarters
12 cloves garlic
½ c. finely chopped fresh cilantro
2 Tbsp. olive oil
1 Tbsp. lime juice
2 tsp. red chile powder
2 tsp. dried oregano
½ tsp. ground cinnamon
1 tsp. fine sea salt

Rajas
4 poblano chiles
2 sm. yellow onions, peeled
½ tsp. sea salt
1 Tbsp. olive oil

Garnishes
cilantro sprigs
lime wedges

wood charcoal for grilling the chicken

Prepare the chicken by poaching: Place the quartered chicken and the garlic cloves in a 5-qt. pot. Add just enough water to cover the chicken. Bring to a boil, then lower the heat and simmer for 20 minutes. Transfer the chicken pieces to a mixing bowl and allow to cool. Remove the garlic cloves and reserve for the Rajas below. (Reserve the chicken broth for chicken soup or discard.)

When the chicken has cooled, pour off any accumulated liquid. Add the chopped cilantro, olive oil, and lime juice to the chicken in the bowl. Toss to coat the chicken. Combine the red chile powder, dried oregano, cinnamon, and sea salt and mix well. Sprinkle this mixture over the chicken and toss to coat well. Reserve and allow to marinate until the charcoal fire is ready.

Preparing the poblano chile rajas: Char the skin of the poblanos over an open flame or under a hot broiler. Seal in a paper bag and allow to cool. Remove the charred skins. Split the chiles open and remove the stems and seeds. Cut the chiles into ½-in. strips.

Cut the onions into ½-in. slices and separate into rings.

Combine the poblano chile strips, onion rings, salt, and the reserved poached garlic cloves from above in a mixing bowl. Add the olive oil and lightly toss to coat the ingredients.

Grilling the marinated chicken: Prepare a wood charcoal fire. Spread the hot coals into a sparse layer. The heat from the charcoal should not be too hot.

Very slowly grill the marinated chicken over the charcoal fire until the skin is lightly browned and the chicken is cooked through. Baste the chicken occasionally with a little olive oil. Transfer the chicken to a serving platter.

Finishing the poblano chile rajas and serving the chicken: Heat a large cast-iron skillet over high heat until very hot. Carefully add the *rajas* mixture all at once. Stir quickly for approximately 30 seconds to 1 minute. Spoon the *rajas* over the grilled chicken. Garnish the platter with cilantro sprigs and lime wedges.

Serve with plain steamed rice or a crisp romaine salad.

Smoked Chile Salsa

MARY SUE MILLIKEN
Border Grill & Ciudad

Yields: 4 cups

1 med. onion, roughly chopped
7 dried chipotle chiles or 3 canned chipotle chiles, stemmed
8 Roma tomatoes, cored
10 cloves garlic
3 c. water
2 tsp. salt
½ tsp. pepper
1 tsp. sugar

Combine all the ingredients in a medium saucepan. Bring to a boil, reduce to a simmer and cook, uncovered, for 20 minutes. The liquid should be reduced by one-third and the tomato skins should be falling off. Set aside to cool.

Pour the mixture into a blender or a food processor. Purée until smooth and then strain. Chill until serving time. Store in the refrigerator up to 5 days or freeze for up to a month.

This earthy, brown salsa is redolent with the heat and smoke of good Mexican cooking. One of my favorites for chips, it's also great on baked potatoes with sour cream, or stirred into chicken soup for instant Mexican pizzazz.

Wilted Spinach Salad with Crispy Sausage

NANCY OAKES AND BRUCE AIDELLS
Boulevard & Aidells Sausage Co.

Serves: 4-6

⅓ lb. Mexican style chorizo or spicy hot Italian sausage removed from casings
1 bunch spinach (about 1 lb.), thoroughly washed and dried
2 c. (loosely packed) bitter greens such as radicchio, arugula, dandelion, or watercress (optional—if not used, double amount of spinach)
½ c. thinly sliced red onion
1 c. julienned jicama root (optional)
½ red or yellow bell pepper, diced

Dressing
1 Tbsp. red-wine vinegar
1 Tbsp. lime juice
1 sm. clove garlic, minced
1 Tbsp. sausage fat
3 Tbsp. olive oil
1 tsp. Tabasco or other hot sauce
salt and pepper to taste

Garnish
1 sm. orange, peeled and sliced into thin rounds

Fry the sausage in a small skillet over medium-high heat for about 10 minutes, crumbling the meat with a fork as it browns, until the fat is rendered and the bits of sausage are crisp. Drain in a sieve placed over a bowl, and reserve 1 Tbsp. of the fat. Place all the greens, well washed and dried, in a large salad bowl along with the vegetables.

To prepare the dressing, pour the vinegar and lime juice into the pan in which the sausage was cooked. Cook over medium heat for 30 seconds and scrape up any browned bits from the bottom of the pan with a spoon. Add the garlic and gradually whisk in the reserved sausage fat and olive oil. Add the Tabasco and adjust salt and pepper. Immediately pour over the salad. Arrange the cooked sausage and orange slices on top, toss well, and serve.

Used with permission from *Flying Sausages: Simple, Savory Recipes for Creating and Cooking with Chicken and Turkey Sausages* (Chronicle Books, 1995).

Sources

Anthony Ambrose

Ambrosia on Huntington, 116 Huntington Avenue, Boston, MA 02116; (617) 247-2400

Refrigerator: Sub-Zero (800-532-7820); Dishwasher: Bosch (800-866-2022); Range: Jade/Dynasty (800-794-5233); Hood: Thermador (800-656-9226); Sink: Franke (800-626-5771); Faucet: Grohe (630-582-7711)

Lidia Matticchio Bastianich

Felidia Ristorante, 243 E. 58th Street, New York, NY 10022-1220; (212) 758-1479; www.lidiasitaly.com

Refrigerator: Traulsen (800-825-8220); Dishwasher: Champion (336-661-1556); Range: Vulcan (800-814-2028); Sinks: Elkay (630-574-8484); Faucets: Chicago Faucet (847-803-5000)

Rick Bayless

Frontera Grill/Topolobampo, 445 North Clark Street, Chicago, IL 60601; (312) 661-1434

Refrigerator: Amana (800-843-0304); Dishwasher: Bosch (800-866-2022); Range: Five Star (216-360-0597); Vent: Viking downdraft; Kitchen Faucets: Chicago Faucet, Soft Flow (847-803-5000)

Paul Bertolli

Oliveto, 5655 College Avenue, Oakland, CA 94618-1583; (510) 547-4382

Refrigerator: Sub-Zero (800-532-7820); Dishwasher: Bosch (800-866-2022); Range: Thermador (800-656-9226); Hood: Thermador; Faucets: Chicago Faucet (847-803-5000)

Terrance Brennan

Picholine, 35 W. 64th Street, New York, NY 10023; (212) 724-8585

Refrigerator: Viking (888-845-4641); Wine Coolers: Viking; Dishwashers: Viking; Range and Hood: Viking; Kitchen Sinks: Kohler (800-456-4537); Kitchen Faucet: Kohler; Butler's Pantry Sink: Kohler; Butler's Pantry Faucet: Kohler; Warming Drawer: Viking; Ice Machine: Viking; Tile: Anne Sacks (503-281-7751); Outdoor Grill: Viking; Cabinets: Christians (212-570-6371)

Cecilia Chiang

Betelnut, 2030 Union Street, San Francisco, CA 94123; (415) 929-8855

Refrigerator: Sub-Zero (800-532-7820); Dishwasher: KitchenAid (800-422-1230); Ovens: Thermador (800-656-9226); Sink: Elkay (630-574-8484); Faucet: Delta (800-428-4330)

Charles Dale

Renaissance, 304 E. Hopkins Avenue, Aspen, CO 81611-1906; (970) 925-2402; www.renaissance.com, www.chefsguide.com

Refrigerator: Viking (888-845-4641); Dishwasher: Viking; Range: Viking; Hood: Viking; Sink: Kohler (800-456-4537); Faucet: Kohler

Robert Del Grande

Café Annie, 1728 Post Oak Boulevard, Houston, TX 77056-3802; (713) 840-1111

Refrigerator: Sub-Zero (800-532-7820); Dishwasher: Bosch (800-866-2022); Range: Thermador (800-656-9226)

Tom Douglas

Dahlia Lounge, 1904 4th Avenue, Seattle, WA 98101; (206) 682-4143

Refrigerator: Sub-Zero (800-532-7820); Dishwasher: Hobart (937-332-3000); Range: DCS (800-777-9109); Hood: Venmar (905-624-0260); Sink: Lambertson Industries (800-548-3324); Faucet: T&S (800-423-0150); Wok: Imperial (800-343-7790); Open Shelving: Metro (800-433-2232)

John Folse

Lafitte's Landing at Bittersweet Plantation, 404 Claiborne Avenue, Donaldsonville, LA 70346; (225) 473-1232; www.jfolse.com

Refrigerator: Viking (888-845-4641); Dishwasher: Viking; Range: Viking; Warming Oven: Viking; Garbage Disposal: Viking; Faucets: Newport Brass (714-436-0805)

Ken Hom

Oriental Restaurant Group plc, 1 Bishopsgate, London EC2N 3AB, England; 33-44-171-929-6868

Refrigerator: KitchenAid Superba (800-422-1230); Dishwasher: Hobart (937-332-3000); Range: Wolf (800-366-9653); Hood: Robert Yick Co. (415-282-9707); Cleanup Sink Faucet: Delta (800-428-4330); Prep Sinks Faucets: Price Pfister (800-732-8238); Wok: Custom, Robert Yick Co.; Duck Oven: Robert Yick Co.; Trash Compactor: KitchenAid

Hubert Keller

Fleur de Lys, 777 Sutter Street, San Francisco, CA 94109-6416; (415) 673-7779

Refrigerator: Traulsen (800-825-8220); Dishwasher: Miele (800-289-6435); Range: Wolf (800-366-9653); Sinks: Franke (800-626-5771); Faucets: Franke

Michael McCarty

Michael's, 1147 Third Street, Santa Monica, CA 90403-5005; (310) 451-0843

Refrigerator: Sub-Zero (800-532-7820); **Dishwashers:** Miele Turbothermic Plus (800-289-6435); **Range:** Thermador "Professional" (800-656-9226); **Downdraft Vent:** Viking (888-845-4641); **Wall Ovens:** Thermador; **Outdoor Gas Grill:** Viking

Frank McClelland

L'Espalier, 30 Gloucester Street, Boston, MA 02115; (617) 262-3023; www.lespalier.com

Refrigerator: Northland (800-223-3900); **Wine Cooler:** Northland; **Dishwasher:** Bosch (800-866-2022); **Range:** Wolf (800-366-9653); **Convection Oven:** Blodgett (800-477-3881); **Kitchen Sink:** Elkay (630-574-8484); **Kitchen Faucet:** Franke (800-626-5771); **Butler's Pantry Faucet:** Herbeau (800-547-1608); **Pizza Oven:** Renato (800-876-9731)

Mark Miller

Coyote Café, 132 W. Water Street, Santa Fe, NM 87501-2137; (505) 983-1615

Refrigerator: Traulsen (800-825-8220); **Dishwasher:** KitchenAid Whisper Quiet (800-422-1230); **Range:** Montague (800-345-1830); **Fryer:** Gaggenau (800-828-9165); **Pizza Oven:** Renato; **Ice Maker:** Ice-o-Matic (303-371-3737); **Sink by Range:** Kohler (800-456-4537); **Freezer:** Traulsen; **Wine Cooler:** Traulsen; **Pastry Refrigerator:** Traulsen

Mary Sue Milliken

Border Grill, 1445 4th Street, Santa Monica, CA 90401-2308; (310) 451-1655; www.bordergrill.com, www.ciudad-la.net

Refrigerator: KitchenAid (800-422-1230); **Dishwasher:** KitchenAid Whisper Quiet Ultima; **Cooktop:** Dacor (800-793-0093); **Oven:** Dacor; **Vent:** Dacor; **Faucet:** Elkay (630-574-8484)

Jean-Pierre Moullé

Chez Panisse, 1517 Shattuck Avenue, Berkeley, CA 94709-1598; (510) 548-5525; www.chezpanisse.com

Refrigerator: Beko (800-887-4226); **Range:** La Cornue (800) 892-4040

Nancy Oakes and Bruce Aidells

Boulevard, 1 Mission Street, San Francisco, CA 94105-1209; (415) 543-6084

Refrigerator: KitchenAid Superba (800-422-1230); **Dishwasher:** KitchenAid Quiet Scrub; **Range:** Montague Grizzly (800-345-1830); **Instant Hot Water Faucet:** InSinkErator (800-558-5700); **Sink in Island:** Elkay (630-574-8484); **Sink in Island Faucet:** Chicago Faucet (847-803-5000)

Patrick O'Connell

The Inn at Little Washington, P.O. Box 300, Washington, VA 22747; (540) 675-3800

Refrigerator: Amana (800-843-0304); **Dishwasher:** KitchenAid (800-422-1230); **Range:** Viking (888-845-4641); **Hood:** Viking; **Sinks:** Elkay (630-574-8484); **Faucet:** Kohler (800-456-4537)

Mark Peel and Nancy Silverton

Campanile/LaBrea Bakery, 624 S. LaBrea Avenue, Los Angeles, CA 90036-3568; (323) 938-1447

Refrigerator: KitchenAid (800-422-1230); **Dishwasher:** Bosch (800-866-2022); **Cooktop:** Dacor (800-793-0093); **Ovens:** KitchenAid Superba

Georges Perrier

Le Bec-Fin, 1523 Walnut Street, Philadelphia, PA 19103; (215) 567-1000

Refrigerators: Sub-Zero (800-532-7820); **Dishwasher:** ASKO (800-367-2444); **Cooktop:** Viking (888-845-4641); **Hood:** Vent-A-Hood (888-327-4663); **Oven:** Gaggenau (gas) (800-828-9165); **Oven:** Viking (electric, convection); **Sinks:** Franke (800-626-5771); **Faucets:** Franke; **Bread Warmer:** Viking; **Plate Warmer:** Dacor (800-793-0093); **Trash Compactor:** Viking; **Hanging Light Fixture:** FlosUSA: (800-939-3567)

Nora Pouillon

Restaurant Nora, 2132 Florida Avenue NW, Washington, DC 20008-1925 ; (202) 462-5143; www.noras.com

Refrigerator: Thermador (800-656-9226); **Under-Counter Refrigerator:** Traulsen (800-825-8220); **Dishwasher:** ASKO (800-367-2444); **Range:** Thermador; **Hood:** Thermador; **Sinks:** Elkay (630-574-8484); **Faucets:** Grohe (630-582-7711); **Recessed Lighting:** Edison Price (212-521-6900)

Anne Quatrano and Clifford Harrison

Bacchanalia, 3125 Piedmont Road NE, Atlanta, GA 30305; (404) 365-0410

Refrigerator: KitchenAid (800-422-1230); **Dishwasher:** Bosch (800-866-2022); **Range:** Wolf (800-366-9653); **Sink:** Blanco (609-829-2720)

Lydia Shire

Biba, 272 Boylston Street, Boston, MA 02116-3917; (617) 426-7878

Refrigerators: Traulsen (800-825-8220); **Dishwashers:** ASKO (800-367-2444); **Additional Cooktop:** Gaggenau (800-828-9165); **Oven:** Gaggenau; **Faucets:** Herbeau (800-547-1608)

Joachim Splichal

Patina, 5955 Melrose Avenue, Los Angeles, CA 90038-3688; (323) 467-1108

Refrigerators: Sub-Zero (800-532-7820); **Dishwasher:** KitchenAid Superba (800-422-1230); **Range:** Wolf Gourmet (800-366-9653); **Kitchen Sink:** Kohler (800-456-4537); **Faucet:** KWC Stainless (888-592-3287)

Alice Waters

Chez Panisse, 1517 Shattuck Avenue, Berkeley, CA 94709-1598; (510) 548-5525; www.chezpanisse.com

Refrigerator: Sub-Zero with custom copper panel (800-532-7820); **Dishwasher:** Bosch (800-866-2022); **Range:** La Cornue: (800-892-4040); **Tuscan Grill:** The Gardener (510-548-4545)